4·95

lucy borodkin

INNER JOU

Shows the unlimited potenti

INNER JOURNEYS

Visualization in Growth and Therapy

by

Eligio Stephen Gallegos, Ph.D.

and

Teresa Rennick, R.N., M.S.

TURNSTONE PRESS LIMITED
Wellingborough, Northamptonshire

First published 1984

British Library Cataloguing in Publication Data

Gallegos, Eligio Stephen
  Inner journeys.
  1. Self-realization
  I. Title   II. Rennick, Teresa
  158'.1   BF637.S4

ISBN 0-85500-189-5

*Turnstone Press is part of the
Thorsons Publishing Group*
Printed and bound in Great Britain

CONTENTS

		Page
	Preface	9
	Introduction	11
Part One	**The Resolution of Long Standing Conflicts**	21
1.	Hold Your Child in Your Lap	23
2.	My Name is Ugly	30
3.	Be a Camera	35
4.	Black, White, and Blue	42
Part Two	**Discovery of the Inner Realm**	49
5.	Ookalok and the Amber Band	51
6.	Inside Church	57
7.	The Jester	62
8.	The Baby King	69
Part Three	**Exploring Relationships**	75
9.	Clearing the Air	77
10.	The Dark Guide	83

Part Four   Overviewing the Self   91

   11. Ina and the Tiger   95
   12. Ivan and the Warrior   102
   13. Wren and Thorne   107
   14. Isol and the Sunflower   113

Part Five   An Esoteric Journey   121

   15. Journey Through the Chakras   123
   16. Guide to Power   136

Part Six   Enhancing Creativity   145

   17. In Your Own Words   147
   18. Sailing the Sea   152
   19. Lev   158

Part Seven   The Book   165

   20. Black Elk   167
   21. Ahab the Arab   173

   Index   187

To Kay and Jerry

PREFACE

The civilizing process has not worked. Certain parts and aspects of people have been denied and negated in the name of society. Rather than enhancing the fusing of what a human being is, there has been a separation. His potential has been sequenced into insulated cubicles and this has resulted in the depletion of his spirit. How can a person be whole without the totality of his mind?

When a person is first born the totality is there, and he exaults in it, honouring his aliveness and creativity. But as we civilize him and force him to respond in certain patterns his aliveness and spontaneity suffer. He becomes a mechanical, predictable being, rather than a creative one.

Many events are currently occurring which involve the uncovering of human potential, but none is more significant than the rediscovery of the use of imagery. The depth, creativity, and wisdom available in each of us, easily accessible through imagery, is a wealth that the world needs for its own growth and maturation.

We wish to express our appreciation to the individuals whose imagery has been set forth in these chapters. Most of the names, and in some cases the events, have been changed to ensure privacy.

We wish also to thank Linda Barnes for typing the manuscript, and Gretchen Gray, Matt Gray, Kenny Enright, and Kay Gallegos for help in its duplication and collation.

Thanks are also due to Mercer University and Oregon Institute of Technology for their support during certain phases of this work.

INTRODUCTION

Visualization, active imagination, guided imagery — whatever term we care to use for this process — takes us to a realm of unbounded richness; to a realm whose reaches were probed by Bosch and Blake, by Swedenborg and Carroll; a realm whose soul is metaphor and myth, and whose progeny is language and logic. But because of our human propensity to territorialize everything we frequently use, and because a territory includes within it the rejection of that which is believed to be the opposite of its core, the imaginal has been characteristically negativized, and such terms as day dreaming, fantasy, and escape have been used in prejudice against it.

In doing this we have cut ourselves off from the very roots of that which makes us *truly* human, blinded ourselves to that inherent richness that makes everyone a king. We have welcomed the practical child, but set its grandparents begging in the streets.

Thinking man's being has been impoverished by adherence to theory about what man is, regardless of whether that theory has its origins in culture, religion, or science. Any theory which purports to define the human being limits him. It is in the nature of theories to be exclusive and therefore limiting. In fact, it is in the very nature of language to define and thus be limiting in its description. From ancient Sparta to modern Russia we have seen social structures imposed on people which thus define those people for a given purpose, whether military or economic. This forces a group cohesion at the expense of destroying the individual, because if an individual is anything worthwhile, he is an originality, and this means an interiority first.

The founders of the United States recognized intuitively the need to allow the free development of this interiority and sought to establish a government which itself was limited, rather than a government which limited its people. And the explosion of inventiveness which followed was evidence enough that this is what is needed for the evolution of the human being. This same phenomenon, the explosive creativity of a people free to develop their own interiority, was seen in ancient Greece and again in that period we call the Renaissance, both of which periods continue to enrich our present lives.

Our current bane is not the government, at least not our government. No. Our current limiting theory comes to us from science, from a science that seeks to define the individual by restricting what is acceptable within his definition; by accepting only those elements of description which fit the previously stipulated conceptual categories of 'objective observation' and 'replicability'. The thing which currently destroys us as human beings is a theory that tells us *before the fact* what is acceptable and what is not. So we define, by exclusion, before we ever describe.

In order to fit man to science John B. Watson[1] threw out consciousness as an aspect of being human, and B. F. Skinner[2] denies the value of feelings. For a long while psychology even excluded the notion of 'mind'. This approach, of seeking to define by excluding, is deadly, regardless of how it is theoretically justified.

The British empiricist, John Locke,[3] considered the mind to be an empty vessel which was gradually filled, beginning at birth, through the sensations and experiences one encountered in living. The doorways by means of which this experiencing entered the mind were the senses: vision, hearing, taste, smell, and touch. These are the same senses that had been postulated two thousand years earlier by Aristotle, who, however, also postulated the existence of a 'sixth sense' which comprised a combination of all five. Aristotle had also referred to the mind as a blank slate, a *tabula rasa*, a term which is usually attributed to John Locke. What Locke did was to put forth a theory, a belief, which came to be taken as gospel: the belief that there is nothing in the mind which has not first been in the senses. He is making an extremely broad jump here, because he is saying that everything we have within has come from without. Something first must have been external before it can become internal. He excludes the validity of the subject. Of course this lent itself well to the developing 'scientific' view, and has, to a greater or lesser extent, dominated Western thinking to this very day.

The modern human being has been stunted and improverished by the perverse imposition of an educational system which has come to view imagery as valid only to the extent that it corresponds to the physical sense-perception of objects. This, also, is an offshoot of 'scientific' theory. Were we truly to recognize ourselves and our origin, we would honour rather than defame.

Our characteristic Western approach to the growing of our children has been deliberately to stunt the mind, to limit it to only a few modes of imaging. Those allowed we call history, memory, art, and a few verbal offshoots of imagery: language, literature, and logic. Within these dimensions we permit, and socially condone, imaging. But we have definite patterns into which we try to mould this imaging, even within these few facets.

Perhaps our true human heritage is the capacity to image, and to image fully. If we use the metaphor of the realm of imagery as a vast, unbounded terrain, we have limited our children to a few toeholds on the beach, a mountain or two, a strip of desert, and a couple of small groves. All the rest is off limits. A few other areas are *known* to exist, but are condemned with great prejudice. The vastness and connectedness of the terrain is never mentioned. The sky is not thought to exist. And we may call a man crazy and view him with horror if he ventures beyond those few encampments which are socially approved. In fact, we fear the rest of the terrain, calling it in most cases 'The Unknown'.

Carl Jung[4] was a man of great heart and courage who dared venture into those forbidden realms. Initially spurred on by the bravery of Freud in crossing those socially defined boundaries, and later saddened by Freud's need to fearsomely impose his own, Jung was a pioneer whose age is yet to come. He did not limit himself to the 'scientific' view that the only data worthy of consideration were those which came through the senses and were then 'made sense of' by the application of logical thought. He did, however, view himself as completely scientific, not in the narrow mode of performing experimental rituals, but in the grand manner of systematically exploring the unknown and reporting what he found.

Jung acknowledged sensing and thinking as two separate channels available to us, but he also recognized two additional channels by means of which our 'knowing' occurs: feeling and intuiting. We have a tradition of considering these latter scientifically invalid. But let us ask the question a different way. Any scientist will readily tell us that the world around is energy in one form or another, and we know by now that our senses are not merely open doorways for this energy, but are filters which both select and organize the incoming energy into perceptual wholes. The understanding of these perceptual wholes led to the founding of Gestalt Psychology. Jung is saying that we have four major pathways for filtering and organizing the energy around us into perceptual wholes, and that the classical senses comprise only one of these.

In venturing into the mind Jung encountered an even deeper organizing sub-structure which he called the 'archetypes'. This term could possibly be translated as 'ancient forms'. What he meant by it was 'seed experiences' which are inherent in the mind. They do not arise from our personal experience but precede it. These are potentialities for experiencing with which we are born, deep systems for organizing our experience into whole elements in our living. A child, for example, is born with a 'mother archetype', a total readiness for experiencing the presence of a mother. The mother he actually meets after birth is not the same as the archetype. The archetype gives him a perceptual mould into which to fit the actual mother, and moulds her presence into a deep and vivid experience. For Jung, experiencing the world becomes an interaction between the individual and his world, and the senses are only one of the passageways through which this interaction takes place.

James Hillman,[5] in his own brilliant way, has carried Jung's work even further in a system he calls 'archetypal psychology'. A very distilled version of his view is that the mind naturally is geared to experience the world by personifying, experiencing everything as a person with its own subjectivity and point of perspective. When our own mind is fully alive we 'experience the world as a psychological field . . . so that the events are experiences that touch us, move us, appeal to us.' Furthermore, there are certain inherent modes of relationship between personifications which are best exemplified by mythology. Our mind, at its highest, is a personifying, mythologizing mind. We take the stuff of our daily lives and live it as if it were a myth, possibly best characterized by the ancient Greek myths but also inhering in mythology in general. In fact, mythology is the spontaneous emanation of these relationships whose origin is deep within the mind. And the way to allow the mind to develop fully, the way of 'soul-making', is to allow the mind its total array of imaging.

My own theoretical approach[6] has been not to try to characterize and describe the contours of that deep realm of the imaginal. It can speak for itself. I have, however, for a number of years been interested in the nature of our attempts to limit what is allowable as a description of this magnificent universe in which we find ourselves, particularly our attempts to limit the description of the Human Being.

The marks that I am making on this paper as I write have their origin in sounds — the sounds of the jungle; the sounds of the howling monkeys standing as a family on the boundary of their territory, announcing their possession. And it is in this function, as a territorial marker, that language was born — language, with all its intricacies, with all of its capacity to lead us to worlds that we have not yet experienced; to send us to do things, not only the projects out of *Popular Mechanix*, but the journey of a Schliemann to the discovery of ancient Troy.

The great paradox is that these sounds, these marks on paper, also have the capacity to confine us to a limited and repetitive realm. These words come to control not only our action, but also our perception, our experience of the world. We each carry within us a lengthy and intricately woven 'map' of what the world is like and how we are to act in that world. A map generated by people but without adequate respect for the deep inherent organizing structures. This map limits the dimension of humankind, and the great task which faces us is to help break apart the map so that each of us can once again claim the integrity and dignity that are the birthright of a Being in the World.

Our great task is to break apart the map which was mistakenly painted by the single origin of our experience of territory and the sounds by means of which we have learned to communicate with each other. This strange conjunction has given us views and descriptions which we then defend, or attack others for, or feel at home within.

Just as the Ringtail monkey has evolved a tail with which he can grasp the limbs of trees, so the human animal has evolved a set of intricate sounds whose function has been successively the delineation of a territory, the maintenance of a social hierarchy, co-ordination during the hunt, the expression of feelings, and ultimately, the reflection of the world experienced. And the grip of its original function is still inherent in our use of language.

We have seldom, in our history, opened up that language to the description of the imaginal, for the imaginal precedes language.

We have been so conditioned to language as youngsters that we quickly learn to respond to the world of human sound in preference to the world of our experience. One of the principal modes of culturization is to set up a situation where the sound and fact conflict, and to reinforce responding to the sound and punish response to the fact. By this means one is gradually weaned away from adherence to experience in favour of adherence to description, particularly where that experience is of the inner realm. We divorce the child from the inner realm so we can subjugate him to the supposed outer. We substitute our control for his. A generation later he asks, 'Why am I in bondage?'

Many systems have emerged, perhaps haphazardly, whose function it is to lead us back to that world of total experience. In their truest sense, these are called religions. We must, however, not confuse them with churches. A church is a system of adherence to the description of a way back. A religion *is* the way back.

This limitation or confinement of description has some well known boundaries. They are the selfsame boundaries which limit an animal's comfort zone, called a territory. This process which prods an animal to establish a territory is the same process which puts limits on the dimensions we are willing to allow our imagery, our language, and ourselves.

An animal establishes a territory with identifiable boundary markers. Beyond this bounding line his first tendency is to run back in fear. On the edge of the boundary he has a tendency to ritualization, anger, and possibly attack, repelling any seeming invader. In the very centre of the territory he is comfortable, and loves, and sleeps.

These three emotional dimensions, fear, anger and love, also characterize the realms of imagery which we allow. There are certain images, patterns of thinking, etc., with which we feel comfortable and which, regardless of their absolute value, we try to perpetuate in our children. If these image realms are challenged or attacked we have a tendency to react stereotypically, or get mad, or attack. We seldom venture beyond this imagery, but when we do we are not fully comfortable, may even be afraid, and everyone has realms of imagery where they are downright terrified.

One of the main things this territorializing of the imaginal does is to give us a defining realm. The person I think of as being 'me' is a realm of images structured with respect to territorial dimensions. This is what has been called the 'ego' or 'self concept', and what we, mistakenly, see ourselves to be. There is nothing wrong with doing this, of course, except that we are never completely comfortable. Such an identification is always a reduction of our true potential; there is always a division between who I allow myself to be and who I really could be at my fullest. And if the territory which defines me is too small the discomfort can be excruciating. In any case, it *is* limiting.

Many people also have the fear, and in some cases a quite intense fear, that if they imagine something then that thing is bound to happen, or, if they imagine themselves doing something, then they will actually do that thing. And maybe they will; but not necessarily. The *fear* of the thought or of the image, however, greatly limits the realm of imagery and the capacity to think. And here let me distinguish between thinking and imagery: thinking involves the use of language. We could say that speaking is thinking out loud. Thinking is venturing in language, usually covertly. Thinking is silent speaking — to oneself or to an imagined other. Imaging is much fuller than thinking, as hopefully this book will demonstrate.

The use of guided imagery as a mode of therapy has a very short history.[7] We are barely on the threshold of its usage. And we should certainly not limit use of it to therapy. Imagery is the rich ground from which human beings grow. It has the potential for growing each of us to our fullest capacity, and its use as therapy is only the first step. Guided imagery or visualization is a powerful technique, and the capacity to visualize grows with its practice. It should be one of the major modes used in education, yet for the most part it is sadly ignored.

In guided imagery, of the sort exemplified in the following chapters, we take a person into those deep structures which allow the inherent organizing process to resume. Originally we see conflicts between what was inherent and what was imposed. Then these conflicts begin to heal and circumstances begin to rectify themselves. Eventually we experience the organizing of organization, integration into a greater unified whole. Through integration we regain our integrity.

The purpose of this book is not to illustrate canned techniques of guided imagery usage, although a few of the early chapters do illustrate this dimension; for an entry to visualization when one has never previously visualized this is perhaps the best beginning. Neither is this a book of instruction for the do-it-yourself visualizer. It has been our experience that the presence of a person guiding the imagery is an essential element, otherwise the imager has a tendency to wander. The person guiding the imagery is like a person on the surface who constantly pumps air to the deep sea diver so that he can breathe underwater. Without him we quickly drown. And he should also know how to pump.

This book is essentially a book of journeys, and it allows the journeys to speak for themselves with very little commentary by the authors. What commentary there is has usually been limited to short notes at the end of the chapter. We could say this is a book of raw data. Yet the data are so rich that they comprise a feast in themselves. This hopefully will serve as an introduction to those who know little or nothing about visualization, and as a small window into the depths and richness and wisdom of that miraculous entity we call the human mind.

Notes:
1. John B. Watson founded the School of Behaviorism which excluded consciousness as a proper subject of study because it was not amenable to scientific observation or manipulation.

2. The modern heir to Watson's Behaviorism, B. F. Skinner, is thought by some to be the most influential man in modern psychology.

3. Locke, J. *An Essay Concerning Human Understanding*. Henry Regnery, Chicago, 1956.

4. For the inexperienced, the only place to begin in understanding Jung's thought is with his autobiography, *Memories, Dreams, Reflections*, Vintage, 1965.

5. Hillman, James *Re-Visioning Psychology*, Harper & Row, 1975. The quotation is from page 130.

6. Territoriality as the substructure of the personality, particularly of the ego, is the subject of a book currently in preparation by E. S. Gallegos.

7. An excellent review of the history of the use of guided imagery can be found in Mary M. Watkins excellent little book, *Waking Dreams*, Harper & Row, 1977.

PART ONE

THE RESOLUTION OF
LONG STANDING CONFLICTS

Visualization is many things. One of them is a precision therapeutic tool. This first part exemplifies its capacity for dealing quickly and potently with an energized conflict.

1.

HOLD YOUR CHILD IN YOUR LAP

It was an emergency walk-in. She was ushered into my office by the secretary, oblivious of being led. Her eyes were streaming with tears. There was a slight limp in her right side. She was frail and tense. I guessed her to be about twenty, although her drawn features and obvious suffering made her seem older. I helped her sit down and the secretary left.

I sat back, settled into my chair, and allowed her the gentle space that she needed. Through her sobs and broken utterances I heard a sorrowful droning.

'I don't know where . . . to begin . . . I feel . . . terrible . . . terribly confused. It's . . . it's Bill . . . he . . . doesn't love me . . . no . . . no . . . I know he loves me. I know it. It's just that . . . that . . . we have such awful fights. He gets so angry . . . but . . . but . . .'

I asked her to take a deep breath and to exhale slowly. She did.
'Once more,' I said.

She did. It was like a deep sigh.

'It's not Bill. It's me . . . ,' she began again, more settled now.

'I want so very much to please him . . . I'd do anything for him . . . but . . . but . . . he doesn't love me . . . No! . . . no

. . . he does love me . . . I know it . . .'

Again I asked her to breathe slowly and deeply which she did.

'As soon as he leaves for work in the morning I start thinking about what I can do for him . . . what I can fix him . . . what he would like for supper . . . And I clean the house thoroughly, thinking the whole time about how pleased he'll be, and how his eyes will light up when he steps through the door and sees how sparkling clean the house is . . . I even polish his shoes and I imagine him coming home and seeing them and telling me I'm the finest wife in the world . . .'

I was aware of the strange intensity in her manner as she said all this.

'. . . And I fix him exactly what he likes to eat. Last night I made him some meat loaf, with breadcrumbs and three eggs and chopped onion, and one clove of garlic, and I glazed it with A-1 sauce, just the way he likes it . . . and the french fries were crisp and golden on the outside and soft on the inside, with lots of butter . . . and I baked a loaf of fresh sourdough bread . . . and . . . and . . .'

Here she cracked, and her sobs sounded as if they were being squeezed out of a deep dark well. Finally she continued.

'. . . All he did was . . . was talk about . . . about his . . . his job . . . at the garage . . . all through supper . . . I waited for him . . . to notice . . . to see what I had done . . . to tell me he loved me. Finally after supper I asked him if he liked what I had cooked and he said it was "fine". Can you imagine? "FINE!" And I told him if he didn't love me and appreciate me I'd just run away and go where they did love and appreciate me and he just looked at me bug-eyed and asked what was wrong and said he did love me and appreciate me and I ran into the bedroom and hid in the closet. Then I heard the door slam and the tyres squeal and I felt really alone and scared . . . I don't know how long I stayed there but I knew I had to be real quiet . . .'

'So your husband left you?' I asked.

'No . . . no . . . he came back . . . later . . . I was real scared . . . he said he was sorry . . . that he did love me and appreciate me . . . he wanted to make up . . . I was terrified . . . we . . . we . . . we . . . made . . . love . . . I . . . didn't . . . feel . . . I didn't feel anything . . . I did whatever he wanted me to . . . but I was real scared . . . I just . . . watched him . . .'

Her face was blanched and waxen. 'How long have you been married?' I asked, as warmly and nonchalantly as I could.

'Almost six months,' she replied, and I felt a slight lessening of her strangulated emotional tone. I felt her become aware of me for the first time.

'Oh, I don't know what's wrong. I really love Bill . . . and I know he loves me . . . I know it . . . but . . . but . . . recently we've been having these awful fights . . . and I snap at him and he says he doesn't know what I want . . . and . . . I'm . . . afraid he might leave me and what would I do, where would I go, there's no place I can go, I don't want to be left alone, I get really scared when I think about that, really scared, and then I think what I can do to make him happy and I clean the house and scrub the floors and polish his shoes and cook him his favourite foods. At first I was really happy. I thought of him as my saviour, like he had saved from from drowning or something . . .'

'Where did you live before you married Bill?'

'. . . with . . . with . . . with Momma . . .'

'Tell me about your mother.'

'. . . she's not . . . my mother. She wanted me to call her . . . Momma, and so I did, but she's not my mother. My mother died when I was two, but I don't remember her. We went to live with . . . with . . . Momma after that . . .'

'We?'

'My father and me . . .'

'And where is your father now?'

'. . . I . . . I don't know . . . Momma . . . Momma was real . . . angry . . . he . . . he . . . he just didn't come home and Momma was real angry . . . and . . . and . . . and Momma said she was gonna throw me out . . . and . . . and I was real scared . . . and I told her I'd be real good and clean house and not be any trouble if only she wouldn't . . .'

'How old were you?'

'. . . five . . .'

'So you were left alone with Momma?'

'. . . no . . . no . . . no . . . it . . . me . . . and . . . and Momma . . . and . . . and . . . and . . . and Hilgie . . .'

'Hilgie?'

'. . . Hilgie . . . Hilgie was Momma's boy . . .'

'How old was Hilgie?'

'. . . H . . . H . . . Hilgie was . . . four years old . . . four years older than me . . .'

Her name was Mercedes but she had always just been Mercy. During the three hours that I spent with her, her story emerged little by little amid sobs and crying and a strange intensity that reminded me of a ravenous animal on the scent. I surmised that, even though unremembered, her early bonding with her natural mother had been good and strong and loving and that this had allowed her to survive as positively as she had, given the traumatic nature of her later childhood.

Mercy's stepmother, a person she never referred to other than as 'Momma', had been a severe and unappreciative woman, although not intentionally cruel. Mercy described her as large and awkward, with legs like stovepipes that did not even taper at the ankle. She was a tight and bitter woman who had no friends and supported the family by working as a school secretary. An element of perfectionism made her precise at her job and also added to her rigidity at home. I could gain no good sense of how long she had been married to Mercy's father prior to his desertion and I wondered if he had not planned the abandonment all along.

Abandoned by her mother through death and her father through desertion, Mercy was determined to do whatever necessary to keep from being abandoned by her stepmother as well. To this effect she became a meticulous housekeeper and an efficient cook, perceptive of her stepmother's slightest annoyance and willing to redo anything with which she found fault. 'Momma', in her tightness, dispensed appreciation seldom and unpredictably but often enough for Mercy to know that it was available, if only she could know how to do the 'right' thing to earn it. The fear of abandonment, however, was always under the thin edge.

By the time she was nine, Mercy had developed a confidence that Momma's appreciation, though grudgingly given, was a constant in her life, but the price was high. It was her childhood.

It was not merely that she performed the duties of a house-keeper. She had essentially become Keeper of the House. Cooking, cleaning, washing, ironing, were done without even a thought that these should not be hers alone. She also assumed the responsibility of informing Momma when anything in the house needed repairs and was usually told to call the company concerned, even to the extent of obtaining different estimates. She developed a vigilance and understanding far beyond her years.

Her assumption of responsibility even extended to Hilgie. It began as part of her other duties: packing the lunch that Hilgie took to school. It then extended to reminding him to wear a sweater or cap when it was cool (at Momma's instigation) or to seeing that he had a handkerchief, and culminated in Mercy staying home from school and nursing him for two weeks when he had the mumps. Mercy hardly got sick herself, and minimized it when she did. Gradually, Momma came to rely more and more on Mercy assuming responsibility for Hilgie's welfare, a task which she undertook with skill in order to avoid arousing any resentment from Hilgie. It seemed that Mercy's keen ability to adapt had earned her a niche of security.

And then it happened. She knew she must have been nine because she was knitting a scarf to give Hilgie on his thirteenth birthday. She was sitting on her bed in her small room, a room barely large enough to hold the small dresser and trunk in addition to the bed. She had just removed the partially knitted scarf and ball of yarn from the trunk where she kept them and had laid them out on the bed. She remembered that she had been trying to estimate how much longer it would take her to finish it, and was counting the days until Hilgie's birthday.

The footsteps were a surprise to her and she barely had time to get the yarn and half-knitted scarf behind her when the door burst open. He tried to reach behind her with both hands and without realizing how it happened she found herself pinned to the bed, almost suffocated by his large, heaving form. Her surprise and fear were jumbled together with the pain and blood in her memory, and it was over before she understood what was happening.

When Momma came home Mercy tried to tell her but she had only uttered a few words when Momma slapped her face, called her a slut and a whore, and accused her of trying to get Hilgie in trouble with her lies. She spent the night hiding in the closet, terrified, jumbled thoughts running through her mind accusingly, what should she have done, where would she go, how could she repair the situation. She couldn't remember how long Momma's brittleness had been sharp and scornful after that, but she know it was a long, long time.

She was sixteen when she met Bill. He was kind and protective, but not very verbal. They were married on her eighteenth birthday.

By now Mercy was emotionally drained. Her raw eyes had been cried almost dry. Although her story had been choked and rambling as she told it, every now and then I saw the glimmer of a connection being made between the patterns of her early childhood and those of her present dilemma.

I asked her to close her eyes, sit back, and take several slow deep breaths. Then I asked that she picture to herself that frightened and lonely little girl that she had been, when things had seemed most hopeless and she felt most completely alone in the world, unloved and uncared for. The image came immediately. I asked her to imagine that she was now holding that little girl on her lap, and had her hold her arms as if she were actually holding someone. I asked her to listen as the little girl told her how sad and frightened and lonely she was, how forlorn and bleak her future seemed, and how she longed for someone to love her. I then told Mercy to imagine herself stroking the little girl's hair and saying to her, 'I am the person for whom you've been waiting such a long and lonely time. I have always loved you, but for a long time I didn't have the strength and understanding to come to you and tell you how beautiful and courageous you are, and how I appreciated your waiting for me. But now I am here and I will always love you and hold you and care for you, and you need never be lonely again.'

I felt a tangible change in the atmosphere in the room, like a warm mist settling. Mercy turned to me, beaming, and said, 'She's smiling! She's smiling!'

I then further instructed Mercy to say to the little girl, 'If you ever feel sad or scared or lonely again, just tell me and I will hold you and love you. I'll always be with you. I'm so glad you waited for me because you're so, so dear to me.' I told Mercy to imagine she was putting the little girl into her heart where she would carry her, and that each day she was to take the girl out of her heart and hold her on her lap, in a rocking chair if possible, and stroke her hair, and tell her what a beautiful little girl she is and how much she loves her. She was also to listen to the girl and let her tell her of how she is feeling and what her needs are.

Mercy, radiant, possibly for the first time in her life, thanked me warmly and left. I never saw her again!

Note:
1.   I had asked Mercy to return a few days later for another session, and, had she been willing, I would have worked with her on a regular basis. As she was an emergency walk-in I had no opportunity to establish ground rules concerning the nature of our therapist-client relationship. I was concerned when she did not keep her subsequent appointment with me as she obviously could have used some long-term therapy, and I would not want the reader to think that a long-standing emotional conflict could be 'cured' by a single visualization.

There are, however, many positive elements about the situation. One dominant one was Mercy's obvious strength and ability to survive and adapt to different circumstances. A second was the love and support that existed in her relationship with her husband. A third was her definite awareness that her conflicting emotions did not fit the circumstances in which she was living with her husband and her need to do something about that. If one views these emotions as the crystallized residue of childhood conflicts then one can deal with that child who felt these, and fulfill that child's actual needs even at this late date. If Mercy followed my instructions to love and communicate with that 'child' on a daily basis, I would predict that her image of the child would change and even grow over time.

The hurt or needy child is a common element in all of us, and visualization is a highly useful tool in helping heal that division between the feeling child that we were and the present adult that we are.

Another positive element was the fact that the conflict in Mercy had reached a peak when she came for therapy, like a highly charged battery, and the current which was permitted to flow in my office, through the imagery, is essentially the energy which feeds growth. Because of the high intensity of the charge one could conjecture that the experienced growth was substantial, although I have no way of verifying that.

2.

MY NAME IS UGLY

Her name was Karen. She would have been attractive had she not been so heavy. Yet 'heavy' is not the right word here, for there was a sense of lightness about her, like a cream puff, a soft rotundity. Let's face it, she was fat. Sweet and fat.

I had known Karen for several years. Her husband was a professor in another department at the small university where I taught. She had come to see me one afternoon in my office, ostensibly to visit, but ultimately to ask me if I would help her with a number of phobias and with some difficulties she had in her marital relationship. I agreed, but only on the condition that she inform her husband and that he be willing to attend some of the therapy sessions at a later date, which he did.

As I worked with Karen I found that many of her phobias had originated as the result of a severe and restricting childhood dominated by the hellfire-and-damnation 'religion' of her parents.

I had been working with Karen for almost a year, seeing her once every two weeks, when one day, seemingly out of nowhere, she said, 'I'm really tired of this weight problem. Is there anything we can do about it?'

I was surprised by this, primarily because it called my attention

to the fact that she had never previously spoken about her weight.
I suggested that we do a visualization about it.

I had her lie back in my office recliner and asked her to close
her eyes and take a deep breath. I then carried her through a deep
relaxation procedure in which groups of muscles are alternately
tensed and relaxed. This leads to a state of deep and profound
relaxation. The actual instructions given to Karen are recounted
fully in the notes to this chapter. [1]

When she was completely relaxed I asked her to imagine that
she was at the entrance of a long tunnel. I suggested that this was
the tunnel of her past, and when she could see herself standing
at the entrance I asked her to enter it and walk along it until she
came to someone or something that would symbolize her 'weight
problem'. After a few moments of silence she said, 'I think I see
it.' I asked her to describe it to me.

'Well, it's yellow and it's square and it's very large. In fact, it
looks like a large cube of butter.' [2]

'Ask it what its name is,' I encouraged.

'It says its name is "Ugly".'

'Ask it what the circumstances were which caused it to first
come into your life.'

After several moments of silence she replied, 'It says that it first
entered my life when I was ten and I started to feel sexual. It says
I was so afraid of those feelings that I would get terrified if a boy
even looked at me, and that it came to help me out by making
me fat and ugly so that no boy would be attracted to me.'

'Explain to it that you are now happily married, that you would
like your husband to find you attractive, and that you are no
longer afraid of feeling sexual. Tell it that you appreciate the way
it protected you back then, and thank it for doing so, and ask
it if it would be willing to leave now that its job is finished.'

'It says yes, it would.'

'Good.'

When I saw Karen two weeks later she had lost seventeen
pounds. She informed me that this had occurred with no effort
on her part, that at meals she would now only eat one serving
and felt no need to eat more than that. Her relationship with her
husband had improved greatly with a new closeness developing
between them.

Notes:
1. Following is a complete transcription of the relaxation instructions given to Karen. This is a standard procedure first devised by Edmund Jacobson (*Progressive Relaxation*, U. Chicago P., 1938).

Concentrate on the feelings in your feet, both feet. I want you to tighten the muscles in them as tightly as you can. Good. Now, when I say the word 'relax', I want you to suddenly release that tightness and let them go limp. RELAX. Good. Now tighten your feet again, as tightly as you can, feel the strain and tension of the muscles as you hold them tense. Good. Now when I say the word, just let them go totally limp and loose. RELAX. Good. Now, once more. Tighten them and hold it. Good. Now . . . RELAX. Good. Now leave your feet relaxed, completely relaxed.

Now tune in to the feelings in the calves of your legs and your knees as you tighten the muscles in them as tightly as you can. Feel the stiffness, the tenseness, hold them tightly for a moment. Now when I say the word, suddenly release the tension, like a string that has been held taut by both ends and is suddenly released. Now . . . RELAX. Good. Feel how loose and free they feel when relaxed, how comfortable they are. Now tighten them again and hold it. Good. Now . . . RELAX. Good. Again, feel the difference, how good and comfortable they feel when relaxed as compared to the tenseness when your muscles are contracted. Now contract the muscles in your calves and knees again, tightly. Hold it and feel the tension. Now . . . RELAX. Feel how good it feels to let them be totally limp and relaxed. Good. Leave them relaxed.

Now the muscles of your thighs and buttocks, contract them tightly. Feel the tension. And when I say the word, just let them go totally limp, like ice that suddenly melts into warm water. Just imagine them suddenly melting completely. Now . . . RELAX . . . Good. Feel how good it feels for those muscles to be relaxed. Now again, tighten them. Good. Now . . . RELAX. Good. And once more. Contract the muscles in your thighs and buttocks tightly. Good. Now . . . RELAX. Good. Now leave them relaxed. Take a deep breath and feel how good it feels to have these muscles relaxed. Your buttocks, thighs, knees, legs, feet. Just enjoy it for a moment.

Now we'll work on the muscles of your stomach, chest, and back all together. You'll see that it's easy to tighten them as a unit. Contract them now as tightly as you can and hold it for a few seconds while you experience how it feels to have these muscles really tight. Now when I say the word, release the tension suddenly and completely. RELAX. Good. Feel how it feels to have these muscles totally limp, relaxed, how soothing it is. Now again. Contract tightly. Hold it. RELAX. Good. Feel it. Once more now. Contract. Now . . . RELAX. Good. Leave those muscles relaxed while we work on your shoulders and arms.

Contract the muscles in your shoulders and arms as tightly as you can. You may feel some muscles in your back and chest tightening also as you do this and that's okay. Be aware of which muscles tighten and of how massive and frozen they feel when contracted. When I give the word suddenly release all of the tightness and contractedness and just let them go limp. Ready . . . RELAX. Good. Feel how good it feels to have them relaxed, to have all that tension disappear. Now once more . . . tighten. Good . . . Now . . . RELAX. Good. And once again, tighten . . . good. And then suddenly . . . RELAX. Good. Leave them relaxed.

And now your hands and fingers. You may feel some of the muscles in your arms tighten as you contract the muscles in your hands and fingers and that's okay as long as you also relax them when your hands and fingers relax. Now . . . tighten them. Feel how frozen your hands and fingers feel when the muscles in them are contracted. Now . . . RELAX. And feel how suddenly good they feel when they relax. You may even feel a slighy tingling in your hands and fingers when they relax, or a very faint vibration. This is their relaxed aliveness. Now once again . . . contract. Good. Now . . . RELAX. Good. Once more now . . . tighten . . . RELAX. Good. Now leave them relaxed.

Now we'll move to the muscles of your neck and jaw. Contract them tightly. Hold it. Feel it . . . Now . . . RELAX. Feel how loose and good they feel, how limp and relaxed. Now again . . . tighten . . . and once more . . . RELAX. Good. The

final time now . . . contract . . . RELAX. Good. Leave them
relaxed.

And now all the muscles of your face: your cheeks, your
nose, your lips and mouth. Your eyes, particularly your eyes.
And also include the muscles of your scalp and ears and temples.
Tighten them really tight, really squinch your face up. Good.
Hold it. Feel how strained and horrible it feels. Now when I
say the word . . . RELAX. Good. Feel how free and loose your
face feels, even flabby. Enjoy it. Now once again . . . contract.
And now . . . RELAX. Good. Once more now . . . contract
. . . and . . . RELAX. Good. Leave them relaxed.

This procedure not only develops an awareness of the difference
between being tense and being relaxed, but it keys the person in
to the signal RELAX, so that relaxation becomes an active response
which can be induced and experienced, rather than merely the
absence of tension.

2.   It is vital to understand that the image need not be a 'person'.
In fact anything at all, symbol, an object, a vaporous spirit, or
even an emptiness, can be the manifestation or guide in a
visualization. Another general observation is that there is a
correlation between the freedom that one allows one's imagery
and the ability to grow and live creatively. One extremely rigid
and bound person with whom I worked would not allow in her
imagery anything that was not allowable in the physical world.
In one visualization she saw herself imprisoned in a brick tower.
She would not allow herself any means of getting out except those
which would have been possible in the physical world, whereas
another person might fly over the walls or even walk through
the wall itself.

3.

BE A CAMERA

When he walked through the door to my office, I could feel the energy. It felt like an inner pressure that had been contained but was ready to explode any minute. His shoulders were powerful but were somehow drawn up behind his neck. His face was ruddy and seething with energy. His eyes intense and penetrating. He was like a very thin balloon, filled with air to the bursting point. The slightest pinprick and he would explode.

I was aware that something needed to be done during this session in order to reduce that inner pressure.

He sat silently and constrained for several minutes.

'I've always hated my father!' he suddenly blurted out. 'He whipped me a lot when I was young. And sometimes he used to stand me up in front of him and just chew me out. And I couldn't answer. I was not allowed to respond. But inside, under my breath I'd be telling what I thought of him, what an asshole he was, how he was the most worthless person on this earth. I'd be burning inside but on the outside I was supposed to show him respect!

'I swore I'd kill him!

'I swore *to God* that I'd kill him!!!'

'Tell me about it,' I said gently, aware that he was close to the bursting point.

'I remember it as if it were yesterday!' he said scowling, his eyes burning. 'We were out in the field, helping my Dad. My sister, Judy, was eight. I was four. I know this because all the children in our family were four years apart and my mother was pregnant at the time. It was a fine spring day and I felt good about helping my Dad. It was the first time I'd worked with him like a man, and I was proud of it. On toward dusk he sent me and Judy home so we could help Ma with the chores. Our house was down the road about a quarter of a mile, and we walked along the side of the highway. I could see the lights of a car in the distance, coming toward us, and for some reason as it got near I ran out in the middle of the road and held out my arms like a policeman stopping traffic. He hit his brakes and I ran back to Judy's side, proud as punch. The car went on but about that time I hear my Dad's footsteps behind and I turn around and he's running after us, mad as a bull. Judy and I took off toward the house with him chasin' us. I ran so hard my shoes came off. As we got to the house, my Ma came out to see what all the commotion was about and my Dad arrived about the same time. There was a big discussion, yelling, and my Dad wanted to know *why* I had run our in front of the car. And I didn't *know* why I had run out in front of it; I had just done it that's all, like I had seen the policeman do in Jacksonville. But he still wanted to know *why* I had done it. I couldn't tell him why. He acted like I had done it just to make him angry, and he was angry. My Ma tried to cool him off but he wouldn't listen to no reason. I was scared 'cause he looked mean and I thought my Ma would cool him off, but after he yelled and asked questions, he went and cut a switch. I'd never seen a switch before. He took me first and turned me over his knee. I was scared and surprised and didn't know what to expect. I'd never been whipped before. And *my God did it hurt*. I thought I'd die. And he wouldn't stop. I yelled and screamed and tried to get away and he'd just whip me harder. I didn't know what to do. I didn't think he'd ever stop. But finally he did but it still didn't stop hurting, not for a long, long time.

'And then he took my sister and whipped her and my Ma tried to get him to stop but he wouldn't and he yelled at her to stay out of it and she got real mad and then went back in the house. After he finished whipping Judy I went over and tried to console her because we were in the same boat. But she was mad as hell at me. She said if it hadn't been for me she wouldn't have gotten whipped, and that it was my fault she got whipped. Then my Dad sent us both inside to go to bed even though it was still early. My Ma asked me where my shoes were so she could go find 'em and I went to bed. And as I was lying there in bed I got madder and madder at him doing that to me and I swore that I would kill him. *I swore to God that I'd kill him!*

'After a while I cooled off a bit and then I realized what I had done and I got real scared. We were Catholics and I had been taught that a thought was the same as a deed and that breaking one of the ten commandments was a mortal sin which would never be excused and if you committed a mortal sin you'd go to hell when you died and be there for eternity. And I knew that eternity was a long, long time. I knew that eternity was forever. So I knew when I died I'd go to hell for what I had sworn and I'd burn in those fires forever. I got real scared then.

'The next morning when I got up I'd kinda forgotten about it, and I wondered why my Dad was being so ornery, and then he reminded me of it, and he told me that from now on I was to do everything he told me without question; I was not to backtalk and I was to do anything he told me immediately or he would whip me again. Well, that set me to burning again. I didn't know why he just couldn't let it go since it was over already but he insisted on keeping it going. And I kept on hating him. The asshole. Everytime I think about it now I hate him a bit more.'

Clem was a freshman in the course I was teaching in Introductory Psychology. I had been aware of him in the large class because of his scowling intensity, but this was the first time he had come to see me in my office. I felt I had to help him defuse this anger. I asked him if he would be willing to experiment with something that might help heal that emotional injury. He said he would, as I knew.

I asked him to close his eyes and imagine that a movie was being made of that old event and that I wanted him to be the camera. In the same way that a camera records any event toward which it is aimed without getting personally involved in the event, just doing its job of recording, I wanted him to imagine that he was

the camera, recording the event, and he was just to tell me what
he was recording. A camera does not take sides. I asked him to
begin at the point where the two children, a four-year-old boy
and an eight-year-old girl, are working in the field with their father.
He took it from there.

'I see the father giving them some small tasks to do, as much
to keep them out of the way as to get something done. The boy
is very proud and works diligently, hoping his father will notice
what a good worker he is. He wants his father to be proud of
him. He seems to be competing with his sister.' (This was said
with some surprise.) 'The boy wants to feel that he is a man like
his father. Now the father is coming over toward them. He's very
gentle and he tells them that it is beginning to get dark and they
need to go to the house because their mother needs them to help
her. The boy is disappointed because he wants to stay out with
his father and do man's work. As they start walking down the
highway the boy is feeling cocky and he wants to show his sister
how much of a man he is so he runs out in the road as a car
approaches and holds out his arms to stop it as he has seen a
policeman do in a nearby town. The driver of the car is surprised
at this and frightened because he almost hits the boy, but he
manages to slow down in time. The boy isn't aware of the danger.
All he is aware of is that his sister needs to see him as a man rather
than as a little boy. He's feeling proud.'

Clem was slow and deliberate in describing all of this, and there
was a sense of him looking inward, becoming aware of aspects
of the situation that he hadn't previously seen.

'The father has continued working in the field after he has sent
the children home. He feels good about them, that they've been
working with him, even though some of it was just to get them
away from home so his pregnant wife could have a rest. Suddenly
he hears a car's brakes squeal and he looks up just in time to see
the car narrowly miss his son in the middle of the road. He leaps
off the tractor and runs to the scene without thinking. It's probably
the fastest he has ever run. But the car keeps on moving and as
it passes the father the driver leans out and yells, "Is that your
damn kid?" The children feel they've done something wrong and
run toward the house. The boy's little feet are flying so fast that
his shoes come off.'

At this point Clem chuckled. It was the first mirthful sound I had ever heard from him.

'The mother's in the kitchen and hears the children yelling. She comes out the back door to see what's going on. She's about eight months pregnant and can't move too fast. She doesn't understand what's happening at first. The children arrive out of breath and frightened and the father arrives a second later. He's scared, excited, and angry. He's in a frenzy. Doesn't know what to do. He's glad his kids are safe but angry that the boy would run out in the road like that. Everybody's energy is at fever pitch.'

Clem is calm as he describes this, very aware that his memory has many dimensions which he had, up until now, not permitted himself to see. I had the feeling that he was waking up out of a dream.

'There is a frenzy of questions: the mother wanting to know what's going on, the father being angry at the boy but hoping he has some excuse which will lessen the tension of the situation, the children flustered and trying to get off the hook, the mother trying to calm the father but his energy is intense.

'Finally he feels that he needs to teach them a lesson and he cuts a switch off a nearby tree. The boy sees him take out his pocket knife and has the fleeting fear that the father *is going to cut him.*' [Clem says this with some surprise] 'He's relieved to see that his father goes over to the tree but then he knows he's going to get a whipping and he tries to hide behind his mother. She's in great conflict, wanting to protect him, yet knowing he has to learn about the danger of the situation, and also knowing that there's no stopping the father once he cuts a switch. She goes back inside and the boy feels abandoned. He's no longer the little man he was earlier in the afternoon. He turns into a whining baby. As the father whips him he cries, yells, and thrashes around. Then the father puts him down and picks up the girl. The boy watches with interest as the father whips her. The father doesn't whip her as hard as the boy, in fact he doesn't want to whip her at all, she's his favourite child, but he feels since she was older she was responsible. The girl is hurt and angry, but she directs her anger at the boy rather than at the father.'

Clem says all of this with growing enlightenment as to the complexity of the relationships in his family, which he had evidently never seen before.

'The girl lies down on a little bench, on her stomach, and the boy goes over to talk to her while the father goes inside to console the mother. The boy feels a comradeship with the girl, like they are united in their pain, united as victims, but she rejects his offer of friendship and he feels very alone, very responsible for all that has happened. Yet he doesn't want to accept full responsibility and blames his father for it all. The father comes outside and orders them both to go to bed. The boy is further angered by this but knows he'd better obey or he'll get another whipping. He goes inside and lies down and the mother comes over to his bedside. He thinks she is going to commiserate with him but she just asks him where he lost his shoes. He tells her and she leaves to go find them. The boy lies in bed. His ass is still hurting. He feels all alone and unloved and thinks it's his father's fault. He lies there getting angrier and angrier at the father, and then the thought occurs to him that he'll get even. He'll kill the father. He's a pugnacious little kid and very determined. He's so angry that he swears to God that he'll kill the bastard. He's not aware that it's his anger that's prompting such an extreme statement, and when he suddenly becomes aware of how extreme it is, he gets very frightened, and all kinds of thoughts about God and religion start running through his head and he gets very *afraid of himself*, afraid of what he might do, afraid of what he has already done, and how he'll be punished for it. At night he sleeps very fitfully; so does his sister. The mother and father have a long talk in bed, the father thinks the boy is being spoiled by the mother, that he's very headstrong and that he needs to be given a new direction or he will get himself killed. The mother knows there's some truth to this, and she's concerned about him and doesn't want him to take any foolish chances any more. The parents don't sleep well. Both are thinking what it would be like if their son had been hit by the car and killed. This is the closest they have come to losing a child and they know how much it would hurt.'

By now it was evident that Clem's identification with the memory had shifted from being identified with an emotionally charged four-year-old boy to an identification with the family as a whole. There was a great change in his manner as he told me this, as well as a greater sophistication in the words that he used.

'The next morning the whole family is on edge. The boy gets up and starts to be his cocky self again but the father cuts him short, determined to shape him up in the only way he knows how. The mother keeps her distance and this surprises the boy because she has always been on his side. The boy doesn't know what to make of it but the anger he feels toward his father burns deep. The father is in error in trying to shift him from being a spoiled brat to being a responsible adult in just one step, and his efforts have the opposite effect. The father doesn't realize that he could help the boy grow up much faster by loving him rather than by being mean to him. A month later a baby sister is born and the boy feels even further alienated. It's like there was a gap in his development which he never got over. He continues to hate his father at every opportunity, but what he really wants is to love him, and for the father to respect him and care about him.'

Clem had carried the replay of the memory farther than I had expected, into events he had not previously described, like the effect of his sister's birth and his continuing anger. When he was done he abruptly opened his eyes as if suddenly remembering that he was in my office rather than re-living the old event. There was a very evident change in him, a new softness, a new depth, a new insightfulness which had not been there before. Even his appearance was changed. The inner pressure was gone. He looked like a relaxed young adult rather than a red-faced child bloated with anger. He thanked me profusely and I told him he had a lot of courage to face what he had faced (and I deliberately left this statement vague and general). Clem finished my course with a new attentiveness. He did excellently in school and is now a graduate student.

4.

BLACK, WHITE, AND BLUE

She was gracious and genteel. Her aristocratic bearing was not of the common, brittle type, but had the warm depths of someone anchored in generations of tradition and belonging, of family, and of the acceptance of responsibility. A sense of quality permeated her dress and bearing. And yet, deep within was an almost imperceptible tender unease which felt delicately balanced on the edge of terror.

She sat quiet and composed following her introduction, and I gathered that in her silence she was both weighing how much of herself she should reveal and assessing me as a potential therapist. I also was in no hurry and comfortably allowed her however much time she needed. And I was aware that I was neither curious nor silently inquisitive as to why she had come, but felt a friendly and warm care for her. Even though she had obviously given considerable thought to what she would say, when she finally spoke her words were direct and spontaneous.

'I've never been seen by a psychotherapist before,' she began, 'and I've encountered considerable apprehension in making my decision to seek your aid. I had you pictured as sharp and aloof, dissecting me like a surgeon and priding yourself at your skill.

So I'm strangely surprised at your gentleness, and I feel I can trust you with what I must disclose of myself.'

We both smiled, relieved that I was only a human being. I knew now that she would go directly to the point, without defence or attempt at subterfuge.

'I'm a whore!' she said suddenly, and I was startled at her abruptness and at a strange discordance.

'I'm sorry,' she said calmly, immediately aware of my sudden perplexity, 'what I mean is I feel like a prostitute.

'I'm in love, deeply in love with a very fine man. When he looks at me, even from a distance, I feel something like an electric current deep inside, and I feel wanton, ravenous, like I could devour him, swallow him whole, like my belly is just oozing out toward him with a will of its own.

'I'm sorry,' she began again. 'It's as if I begin to lose control, and then I get flustered and have difficulty getting enough oxygen.' Her face was red and taut. 'And then I begin thinking that I'm a prostitute for feeling this way, and I know I've sinned, and I resolve to remain chaste and pure as I should be. Then I begin to feel a battle rage within me and I know I must be strong and resolute and adhere to the higher ideals and resist temptation!' This latter was said with a straight and militant bearing, and I began to feel the power parameters of her struggle as she divulged it.

I asked her if she had ever made love with this gentleman. After a hesitant silence she told me she had.

'Twice! . . . *and it was glorious!*' I contained my amazement at the power and fullness of this exclamation and listened calmly while she continued. 'I've never felt anything so deeply in my life. Nothing. I shuddered from my very core. It felt like a seizure, although I've never had a seizure. *I was seized.* I was possessed. I felt a communion with him. We were continuous with one another. I seemed to have melted and become fluid, with no structure of my own. I shudder even remembering it.'

She became abruptly silent and strained, vigilant, as if anticipating a reproach from somewhere.

'How beautiful,' I said softly.

'But it's not, no, *no*, I shouldn't feel that way, it's wrong, it's sinful. I need to be strong. I *must be strong.*'

Barbara had grown up on a large estate as the only daughter of a wealthy family that prided itself on its noble origins. Her father was a powerful man who skilfully controlled the family businesses and investments. From her childhood she remembered him as hearty and robust, as a man whose life she enriched and whose aliveness filled her own. There had been a deep emotional connection between them until Barbara was eleven at which time he became cold and aloof, distant and suspicious, although no singular event appears to have precipitated this apparent rejection. She had never been able to understand how she had failed her father.

Her mother was a lean and gaunt woman, much occupied with religion, and was given to bouts of depression and endless sequences of physical ailments whose only cure, after extensive medication and consultation, appeared to be displacement by a new ailment.

She had three brothers, all engaged in one capacity or another in the family business, with whom her relationship seemed to be primarily formal and social.

And much of her early education had come from a severe and uncomprising governess who seems herself to have lacked any childhood, was rigid in her morality, and belonged to her mother's church.

Barbara had been married for ten years to a man not unlike her early governess, a man who lived in terms of duty and obligation, a man whose social aspirations were kept tightly and bloodlessly secret (or so he thought). Their relationship was both loveless and soulless but it presented a pretty picture. At least until their divorce.

Dissolving her childless marriage to her husband had been enhanced by the feelings that Robert aroused in her. It was as if he had awakened something in her that had been too long asleep. Although she had always honoured her marriage vows to her husband, and would probably have continued to do so for the rest of her life had she not met Robert, she began to understand their emptiness together the moment she felt that deep and frightening something that Robert's look evoked in her. It was a look which made her hunger deeply, a hunger with an aliveness of its own, and which was profound and awesome, itself devouring and longing to devour. It was not that her attraction to Robert had caused her to leave her husband. That was too simple and superficial. It was more that an aliveness was ignited in her whose power and vibrancy was just too great for that brittle superstructure she had called a marriage, and it had shattered like an eggshell exploding from within.

But then there was the guilt. Although its abrupt appearance was always unpredictable, it seemed to spring at her whenever she became aware of savouring her deep and rich aliveness, of enjoying her profound feelingness. It was like the sudden whack of a ruler followed by intense self-recrimination, severe self-chastisement and exhausted repentant confusion.

I asked Barbara to close her eyes and make herself comfortable in the recliner where she sat and I took her through a procedure designed to induce deep relaxation. When she was sufficiently relaxed, I asked her to remember the feeling she had whenever Robert looked at her.

'Yes, I can see him looking at me and I immediately get the feeling that I have when I see him,' she replied.

'I want you to feel that feeling and then just watch as it turns into an image. Don't try to do anything but just allow the feeling to turn itself into an image that can represent it. Don't you select the image. You just watch. Let the feeling select the image,' I said.

'I see a woman dressed all in black. She has a hood on and I can't see her features. She's moving her body very suggestively,' she replied almost immediately.

'Good. Now, just let that image be there for a moment, and I want you to remember the guilt you sometimes feel, and the way you criticize yourself, and condemn yourself.'

'Yes, I'm feeling that way now,' she replied after a pause, and I saw the muscles in her face tense slightly.

'Very good. Now I want you to allow that feeling of guilt and self-chastisement to turn itself into an image also. Allow it to select any image it needs to adequately represent itself. You just observe and tell me what the image is.'

'Yes . . . it's a woman dressed all in white. She also has a hood so I can't tell you what she looks like, but she's standing very stiffly. She seems to be standing rigidly at attention,' Barbara answered.

'Good. Now, in your imagination, I want you to let the woman in white and the one in black stand apart from each other, at a distance that feels comfortable,' I continued.

'Yes, they're standing a distance apart, but they're very aware of each other's presence.'

'Good. Now I want you to allow a third image to appear. Again, don't even try to do anything, just allow. This is to be an image of someone who understands and is in touch with them both. Someone who can tell you about them, and about their relation to each other.[1] Allow this third image to appear of its own accord. Don't you *do* anything.'

'There is another woman there now. This one is dressed in blue, a light blue, and she's very big. She also has a hood, so that I can't see her face, and she has one hand touching the head of the black lady and the other on the head of the white lady. She's standing in between them and they're only as tall as her waist.' Barbara was completely involved in the vision.

'Ask them what their names are,' I said.[2]

'The one in white is too stiff to answer, and the one in black is just constantly moving and this seems to preoccupy her so that she can't answer. The one in blue says, "My name is Woman".'

'Ask the one in blue to tell you about the relationship between the other two,' I said.

'The one in black is moving all around, really wildly now, jumping up and down, dancing around,' Barbara said with some concern, 'and now the white one seems to be getting tighter and tighter but there seems to be something moving inside her.[3] Now a lot of little women dressed in black are coming out of the white one, like they're being squeezed out of her, and the white robe falls flat and empty on the ground. All the black women are jumping up and down together, except that now their clothes have changed colour, they're all wearing different colours, bright colours, and there are children with them, and they're all dancing happily,' Barbara said excitedly.

'What's the woman in blue doing?' I asked.

'She's moving out into the midst of those that are dancing. Then she kind of sinks down into them and then she rises up again as they dance around her. They're all happy. They're all enjoying themselves. They're all very alive. They're celebrating!'

Barbara was radiant as she came out of this experience. The edge of terror was gone. There was something wholesome and alive about her. She thanked me and left.[4]

Notes:

1. The introduction of a third party that is in touch with both sides of a conflict is a highly functional technique for resolving conflicts and was devised by Dr Arden Mahlberg. It is the subject of an article by him which is currently in preparation.

2. I find that the names given by images are always significant, usually profound, sometimes astounding, and occasionally humorous.

3. Visualization usually has its own life, and will occasionally spontaneously go in its own direction, even in opposition to the person doing the visualizing or the person guiding it. It is important that this be understood and allowed when it takes place.

4. Subsequent sessions with Barbara indicated that her conflict concerning her relationship with her lover had indeed been resolved. They eventually married and have a warm, rich communion.

PART TWO

DISCOVERY OF THE INNER REALM

This section illustrates the surprise of discovering the inner realm with its wisdom and lucidity. Such a discovery can change a life, bringing it depth and beauty. It is akin to finding a long lost friend without whom one's life would always have felt incomplete.

5.

OOKALOK AND
THE AMBER BAND

I had known Raoul for about a year. He had come to the university as a highly motivated and aspiring Assistant Professor of Biology. It had been easy for us to meet because of similarities in our cultural backgrounds and because we both spoke Spanish. Even so, we were not close friends. In fact, I don't believe Raoul had a close friend among the faculty at that time. There was something about him that made it difficult to develop a smooth interaction, an intensity and brittleness in his manner, a tendency for him to play a role of macho one-upmanship, a certain intrusive awkwardness in his communication.

But he was a brilliant biologist and my interests in animal behaviour and territoriality drew me toward him, and we shared a mutual familiarity with the research and writings of the ethologists, particularly Tinbergen and Lorenz. I came to learn that Raoul had a strong interest in the inheritance of ritualized behaviours, such as the courtship and nesting ritual of many species, and it was on this ground that we met.

Over time, as our conversations broadened, I told him of my interest in mental imagery. His own view of imagery was the typical scientific view that the function of images is to provide

51

a representation of the world we experience. Thus he could 'see' his biological specimens when we discussed them over coffee, or his classroom, or the movements of the Greylag geese described by Lorenz but which he himself had never seen. But when I brought up the topic of the deeper function of imagery, of mental elements which have an intelligence of their own and from which we can learn, Raoul was highly sceptical. He viewed all imagery as subordinate to the intellect and thus whose job it was to 'reflect' one's thoughts. To him imagery was a kind of slave or servant.

When I proposed that the mind was a vast realm peopled by great varieties of images of which memory and logic were only two minor facets he remarked that I was lost in fantasy. I replied that fantasy was also one of those facets by means of which the mind shows us its vastness and that there were many other facets which were totally unknown to most people. At this point he challenged me to show him them. I accepted his challenge.

I knew he was caught. His own defensiveness had provided the challenge, and he was caught between his need to grow and his propensity to defend what he 'knew'. I knew he was allowing me the opportunity to carry him beyond his 'knowledge', that which he thought was the only source of the unknown: books, teachers, and his own scientific experience.

We moved to my office and I had him stretch out on the recliner.

'Close your eyes and take a deep breath,' I instructed without hesitation. He did.

'Feel the contact that your body makes with the recliner . . . and imagine the contact that the recliner makes with the floor of this office, and that this building makes with the earth.

'Now become aware of the rhythm of your breathing, the inhalation . . . exhalation . . . inhaling . . . exhaling good, very good.

'Imagine that as you inhale your breath goes all the way down into your feet, and imagine also that your feet are like balloons, so that as you breathe into them they fill up and expand, and as you breathe out they deflate and collapse, completely relaxed. Feel them as they alternately expand and relax. Good.

'Now imagine that as you breathe your breath goes directly into the calves of your legs and that they also are like balloons so that as you breathe in, they fill up with air and expand and as you breathe out, they deflate and collapse. Watch them in your imagination as they alternately fill up and relax. Good.

'Now breathe directly into your knees and see them expand like small balloons, and then relax, totally limp, like a balloon with no air.

'Now your thighs. Breathe directly into your thighs and watch them expand and relax, in your imagination.'

In this manner I carried Raoul through his pelvis, his back, shoulders, arms, hands, fingers, chest, neck, and through all the parts of his head and face, slowly, gradually, keeping an eye out for signs of tension in any of these areas and concentrating on those areas where the tension occurred.

'Now breathe into your eyes, and into the muscles of your eyes, and into the area surrounding your eyes, particularly the backs of your eyes, filling them up and relaxing them deeply, deeply.

'Now imagine that your entire body is like a balloon, and that as you inhale the air goes directly to every part of your being, and as it does your entire body is energized and deeply relaxed. Good.'

I had now carried Raoul through the entire relaxation procedure and he was deeply relaxed and comfortable. It had taken about forty-five minutes.

'Now allow there to be an open place for your imagination, a clearing, a place of stillness.

'Now . . . in that opening in your imagination allow there to begin to appear the place where you need to go to meet someone who can tell you things about yourself that you haven't known before. Don't try to make anything happen. Don't even make an effort. Just be alert and describe to me what you see in your imagination. Just allow the place to be there.' I said this quite firmly.

'What's happening, Raoul? You can talk to me without disturbing your state of relaxation.'

'It's not going to work. All I see is white. Just a lot of white, like white hills or something,' he said, and I detected a note of dejection in his voice.

'And where are you in these white hills? Can you see yourself?'

'. . . Yeah, I'm just standing there looking at the white hills,' he replied.

'Look closely at yourself and tell me what you're wearing there,' I said.

'Oh . . . I have a thick coat on . . . with a big furry hood
. . . the coat is soft with fur on the inside . . . and I have pants
like that, too . . . and gloves and shoes . . . it's cold . . . that white
stuff is all snow . . . snow everywhere you look . . . and I'm dressed
like an eskimo!' This was said with an element of surprise and
discovery.[1]

'Look carefully around the landscape and see if you can see
anything else,' I encouraged.

'. . . Yes, I see something off to my left . . . it looks like an igloo
. . . and there's someone standing by it . . .'

'Go up to that person. What does that person look like?'

'. . . He's dressed in furs, like me, but he's wearing a wooden
mask . . . it's very stern . . . and has little strips of fur for eyebrows
. . . I'm walking toward him . . . he knows I'm afraid of him
. . . as I get right up to him he takes off his mask . . . he's smiling
. . . he has a very round face and is very alive and healthy
. . . he's a man . . . but . . . his face looks like that of a child
. . . he's very alive and expressive.'

By now Raoul was totally engrossed in the visualization. 'Ask
him what his name is,' I said.

'. . . He says his name is . . . Ookalok . . . he says it sounds
similar to catalogue . . .'

'Ask him what he is here to tell you or show you.'

'. . . He says I've been living my life like a spaghetti and I should
be living it like a juicy steak . . . he laughs and laughs as he tells
me this . . .' Raoul himself was chuckling as he described this to me.

'. . . He says I am too concerned with rules . . . he says I act
as if everything I do or everything I feel should have a rule to
govern it . . . he says I am misusing my capacity to make rules
. . . he says rules are like guidelines rather than like commandments
. . . and that I am applying them much too broadly in my life
. . . he says they should be helpful, like tools, rather than things
that interfere with the flow of living . . .'

At this point Raoul emitted a deep sigh and a single tear began
rolling down his cheek.

'. . . Now . . . he's showing me a time in my childhood . . .
I was maybe four or five . . . it was a time when my father was
out of work . . . and so . . . he was home a lot . . . he's also very
angry . . . I see him spanking me when I misbehave . . . only I

didn't know I had misbehaved . . . it's almost like he lies in wait for me to do something wrong and then he pounces on me and punishes me . . . I didn't understand why he was punishing me so much . . . whenever he punishes me he tells me of a rule that I broke . . . I begin to feel that the world is made up of rules and if I can only know them all then I will be safe from more punishment . . . but it also seems like an endless job to learn all the rules . . . but I'm a determined little kid . . .'

By now tears were streaming freely.

'. . . Oh . . . I just realized that I'm standing there with Ookalok watching all this . . . Ookalok tells me that that was the time when I first got stuck on rules . . . that it was a matter of survival at the time, but that was only because my father was so punishing . . . he tells me that my father was very upset because he had lost his job, but I didn't understand that aspect of it at the time . . . wow . . . I don't think I had ever thought about that situation . . .

'. . . Now he's taking me into his igloo . . . we go down some steps . . . inside there are some furs on the floor . . . he has three children . . . a daughter who seems to be about twelve . . . a boy about eight . . . and a young child . . . his wife is there, too. He's pointing at something . . . they each have something . . . like a beam of light only it's like a deep golden brown . . . a deep amber . . . and it seems to be coming right out of their stomachs . . . or out of the middle part of the body . . . they are all connected together by these bands. Ookalok is pointing to the amber band . . . and he tells me, "This is what living is about . . . when these connections are strong and rich then some rules may emerge from them but no amount of rules can ever create this, and this is what living is about . . . Many people think our life is bleak and empty way out here . . . but the landscape enriches us by making us extremely aware of these connecting bands, and it is these that make us rich, it is these that make us wealthy." I am suddenly aware that they are all glowing from within . . . it seems like these connecting bands somehow ignite them inside . . . they are vitally alive and glowing with that life . . . he's taking me back outside now . . . he's wishing me well . . . he comes up close to me and says very definitely "Look for the amber band!" Now he's putting his wooden mask back on.'

'Thank him for being your guide,' I said, 'and then find your way back to this room with me by the best route available, and when the time is right, gently open your eyes.'

Notes:

1.   Mention should be made here of the fact that Raoul had never been to any similar landscape, and also that this was in contrast to the desert country where he had spent his youth.

2.   The integrity of visualization is itself a fascinating topic. The entire visualization appear to exist as an integrated whole from the beginning, even though its aspects emerge sequentially, one at a time.

6.

INSIDE CHURCH

I did not see Raoul for several days following the visualization, and had not known what his reaction would be. I knew it was possible he would entrench himself, even further in his well-structured intellect, defending his past and rejecting the visualization as a moment of 'fantasy' or even 'insanity'. So I was pleased to see his eyes light up when we met a few days later.

He had been deeply moved. Some key elements in the way he perceived himself had changed. He had also become much gentler in his interactions with others. A sharp edge in him had softened.

He was also hungry. I had given him a taste of growing from within and it had whetted his appetite for more. I had been the source of his contact with a deeper element which directs our growth and allows a brief taste of fulfilment. All of his striving in the world, from the initial relating to his father by trying to learn the 'rules', to ultimately obtaining a Ph.D. and becoming a university faculty member had been fuelled by his need to grow. He had utilized what guidance and direction was available in his world for this growth, but it had been sadly one-sided. Now he had tasted the other shore, and his natural intelligence and intense motivation made him hungry for further exploration.

He asked me if I would 'take' him on another visualization. There was something which had troubled him for a long time, and although he had intellectualized it and stored it away in a pigeonhole, something about his previous visualization had reawakened it, and it was again nagging at him.

He was perplexed about the place of the church in his life. He had been raised in a very stringent religion which was central to his culture, had learned dogmatically to obey its rules, but was always ill at ease in his relationship to it. When he first had entered the university he had tucked it away and avoided thinking about it, instead devoting himself as much as he could to scientific pursuits. Now his old perplexity had rearisen, and he wanted to know if a visualization could help him understand.

We retreated to my office, and again I had him relax in my recliner.

'Allow your eyes to close and take a deep breath. Imagine that your body is a balloon, and as you become aware of the rhythm of your breathing, imagine that your entire body is filling up with rich, fresh air and is then relaxing completely, with all the tension leaving. Good.

'Become aware of the contact that your body makes with the chair, and imagine that your body is growing roots down through the chair and deep into the earth. Allow the roots to grow as big and as extensive as you wish. Imagine the little rootlets burrowing around in the rich earth, seeking out places of moisture and nutrients which they then soak up and transport up through the roots into a tender little shoot that is just breaking through the surface of the earth.

'Allow that green shoot to grow from the moisture and nutrients that are being carried to it, and let it grow big and tall, putting out leaves as it grows. And then as it stands in the pure sky, underneath the sun, allow a small bud to appear. Watch as the bud gets larger and larger and then allow the bud to blossom, opening up its petals and breathing in the sky and the sunshine.

'When you can see this happening, tell me about the flower.'

After a few moments of silence, Raoul replied, 'I saw a white bud that looked like it might be a white tulip, but then as it opened up I saw there were many more petals than a tulip has, very firm petals, and they unfold very rapidly. They seem to continue to grow very rapidly from the centre. It's a very large flower, unlike any I'm familiar with, and the profuse growth of petals calls my attention to the centre of the blossom. I expect to see the stamen and pistals, but they're rather unclear, and as I look closer I seem to see a little village in it. [1]

'The little village seems to be snow covered, blanketed with white, but with bright, sparkling lights in the windows, which are made by yellow, glowing fires inside. Smoke is coming out of the chimneys. It's a cozy little village way off in the wastes, way off in the mountains. It's like an alpine village in wintertime, [2] with smoke swirling up from the chimneys.

'I am in the town and I am wearing knickers and high wool stockings, a little cap like a Tyrolean cap, and a short jacket. It is olive green and gray, with black piping.

'It feels like a little Tyrolean or Austrian village. Very cozy. I am alone on the streets and I'm going uphill. Cobbled streets. There's a church at the top of the hill with a steep spire.

'As I get up toward it, I realize there is a gathering going on inside, a community gathering. There's a warm feeling from the inside, and also the noise of people who have gathered together warmly.

'I start to go inside but something seems to say, "No," and instead I go around to the back of the church, and enter through . . . the sacristy. It's a room with the vestments of all the priests. And I go through there and come in.

'Some kind of service is going on. And it's as if I'm there, but also as if I'm unseen. I'm there as a visitor, kind of invisible in a way, just watching what goes on. Thee's a priest saying mass, all dressed up in his robes, white and gold, giving communion. And a lot of villagers in the pews.

'It's a very warm gathering. Everybody's . . . everybody there has a warm, rich heart. They've gathered together in quiet celebration.

'I go up to the priest and I ask him what I'm supposed to learn, and he tells me just to watch. And there seems to be some kind of general spirit there, a very big, warm spirit that everybody's attuned to. Kind of a single being, like a great big egg. And everybody's attuned to that single being which is . . . of which they are a part. Each one of them is like a unit of the being, and yet it's bigger than all of them put together. It's as if there is just one organism of which each one of them is an aspect, and each one is honouring, tuning in, to that greater being. And the priest is there just kind of to unite them, guide them, so they can do it with a singularity of mind.

'And it's as if that being has a head a body, just like a person, and each of the villagers is an aspect of the body, and the priest is an aspect of the head. And the church itself is a reflection, just a reflection, of the structure of that being. And the being indicates that even though we use symbols which point up into the sky representative of it, that really it is something very infused in the earth. The earth is really where its heart is.

'Everybody there is breathing in unison, and as they do, the being itself respires.

'In acknowledging and respecting that greater Being they also acknowledge and respect the connection that they have with each other, the fact that they are not separate entities, but because of that greater Being, they are connected. That greater Being is their connection with each other. And it's evident that it doesn't matter what the service is, as long as it aims at reminding people of that greater Being and of the connection they have. And in that same sense then, a play, or a symphony, or a football game, is also a religious performance, in the sense that it points to a . . . a unifying factor. And that the evident thing in any situation is to be aware of that unifying factor, in any situation that involves other people, to be aware of that unifying factor. And when one does that, one is then very aware that one is not separate from those other people. And that the evident thing in our relationship is that we become very aware of that unifying element by means of each other.

'And then the understanding comes through that Hell is the belief that we are individuals, separate beings. And that to be holy is to live from the standpoint of that connectedness. It's as if we are individual fingers which are united by a hand, and who have become unaware that there is a hand there.

'I start to ask the priest a question and he tells me, "Just watch, just watch, just observe."

'So I settle myself down in a little niche on the altar and am just aware.

'And it's as if in communion the host really is a host and that it represents the host of which we are all guests.

'Now I see the village once again from a distance and I see that what makes it a village, and also what makes it so cosy, is a connectedness that hovers over it. Just like a cloud but kind of like a clear cloud that hovers over the village. Also very much like a nest.

'And then I see myself once again on the outside of it looking in, into that white blossom.'

Notes:

1. The spontaneous movement from my guidance to his own setting is quite fascinating and perhaps indicative of the centrality of the question he is seeking to have answered.

2. It's interesting how again the setting seems to be the opposite of that where Raoul spent his childhood.

7.

THE JESTER

A beautiful deepening was taking place in Raoul. A soft radiance had replaced the previous social jaggedness. He had been awakened to a new dimension within himself of which he had previously known nothing. Others around him felt the change although they were at a loss to describe it. Raoul was developing a respect for his own inner dimensions, and he also looked at others, now, with an appreciation of what they contained within even if they themselves had no knowledge of it. He was beginning to see the indescribable richness which was buried deeply and covered over.

Our conversations together took on a new meaning, and occurred now at a different level. But then a new preoccupation arose quite suddenly. The President of the university had retired and after a lengthy search a new one was hired. The new President brought with him a new Dean of the Faculty who initially appeared bright and eager, but whose haste in attempting to institute his own ideas quickly alienated many of the faculty. His attempts to restructure the Division of Biological Sciences, which included the Departments of Biology, Physiology, Anatomy, and Veterinary Medicine, brought him into direct conflict with the

Chairman of the Biology Department who promptly resigned in protest (and who would have retired within two years anyway). This brought Raoul into conflict concerning what action he should take as he firmly supported the Biology Department Chairman but could also see the long range value of some of the new Dean's proposed changes.

One day he came to me, dejected and perplexed, and asked if a visualization could possibly help him understand what action he should take in the situation. I agreed to help him with a visualization of a guide who could possibly give him some advice about it.

I asked him to sit in my office recliner and relax. By now he could relax completely with little prior preparation. I asked him to picture a large screen and to allow the number 100 to appear on it.

'When you see the screen with the number 100 on it clearly, begin to let the numbers change in reverse, sequentially, one by one. From 100 to 99 to 98 and so on, until the numbers suddenly disappear. Tell me as soon as they disappear.'

Raoul was silent for a while and then said, 'They've disappeared.'

'What was the last number you saw on the screen?'

'Seventy-seven.'

'Good. And now there's going to appear right in front of your eyes the scene where you're going to meet a guide who can help you understand your present situation. Allow the scene to appear.'

'Yes, I see very tall trees, they're poplars, and they're growing on each side of a road or path that goes straight ahead and disappears in the distance.'

'By these trees, and by this road, a figure's going to emerge, the guide who will help you understand.'

'Yes, I see a jester . . . all dressed up like a jester.'

'Good. Let him approach you . . . tell me when he's right there.'

'He is with me.'

'Describe him to me.'

'He has a smile on his face. Tremendously deep penetrating eyes. He's dressed in a jester's cap and costume, multi-coloured, like in the English courts, and a bell on the end of his cap. There's something devilish about him.'

'What is it that's devilish about him?'

'The look in his eye.'

'Tell me about it.'

'It's as if he's very knowing. Rather than using his knowledge seriously he can use it in any way he needs to. He's about my size but he seems remarkably . . . he seems like he's bent over but he's also remarkably agile, as if his muscles are free to move in any way they need to.'

'Why is he bent over?'

'No reason. It's just his stance. It's almost as if to make himself smaller.'

'Does he know why you've come?'

'He says that I've come for many reasons.'

'Ask him what you need to know.'

'I told him that I came to talk to him about how to deal with the situation involving the Chairman of the Biology Department, and I aked him if he could advise me about it and he said, yes, he could, but that I've also come to talk to him about the way that I deal with situations in general in my life.'

'And what do you do now?'

'We kind of amble around on the path. It seems like any direction is possible on the path. My own sense is that I'm directed straight ahead. He has a lot more flexibility than I do. He dances all around me, from side to side, in front and behind.'

'What is he showing you?'

'He's showing me freedom, and that I have an intellectualized view of the path, which is linear. And he's showing me that the path is not linear. He tells me that I typically deal with situations by holding off doing anything until the situation resolves itself and I won't have to act or even take a stand in it. That I stand on the sidelines and just watch. And he's indicating to me that I can play with situations, that I don't have to take them constantly seriously. Even if they're serious situations I can still play with them, see them from all sides, enjoy them from all of the sides. He tells me that avoidance of my anger is what's kept me so straight. And that there's a beautiful depth and humour to my anger. The energy involved in my anger is the same energy that's involved in humour.'

'Do you need to ask him about this?'

'He says that I'm taking the Dean and the Chairman far too seriously, and that I need to see them as clowns. If I enter into the situation myself, seriously, I should do it with a touch of humour. And that their seriousness about it is one of the humorous elements. And that my own seriousness is also humorous. He tells me that when a thing is extreme, that in itself makes it humorous. That life is so full and rich and bountiful that to concentrate totally on any single facet is a very humorous thing in itself. It's like getting stuck somewhere. Like Brer Rabbit and the Tar Baby. He takes the Tar Baby so seriously that he gets stuck to it and that's what makes the whole thing so funny. He says that humour is a great dissolver. It's like a solvent for the glue that gets us stuck to any particular situation. He says that it's funny that I'm even taking *him* so seriously, listening to him as if he has great words of wisdom. He takes me by the hands now and gets me to dancing around with him.' (Raoul suddenly begins to laugh.) 'He's showing me that I'm even taking the dancing seriously. He says that this is almost like a sickness that I have, taking things seriously.'

'Ask him the reason.'

'The sickness is a constriction of vision. He uses the image of a camera aperture that is cranked down to a fine pinpoint and has lost its flexibility. It should be able to open up totally or close down freely, spontaneously, like the pupil of the eye. And he says that my sense of myself is fixed in that very small aperture. And if it opens up wider the sense of who I am would dissolve.'

'And then what would happen?'

'He says then I would swim without boundaries. I ask him if he can help me bring back its flexibility, and he says, "That's what we're doing right now."

'He's showing me that the image of myself was fixed when I was five years old and feeling very sorry for myself and very angry, and holding both of these attitudes very seriously. I was taking my father and his rules very seriously.

'He just flung me over his head and I realized suddenly that we'd been only dancing in two dimensions. And he points out that there are even other dimensions. He says that there's a dimension of running something into the ground and that most of us spend our lives doing that. He says that whatever it is that we do, even if it's a very narrow thing, if we do it with a touch of humour that helps loosen it. He says humour always involves broadening of perspective rather than narrowing.

'We're dancing around rather wildly. It feels quite chaotic. I've started flinging him around now. We take turns, like two acrobats. There's a tremendous amount of skill involved in what he's doing and what he's showing me. It's not just a haphazard thing. Marvellous co-ordination! We're throwing each other over successively so that we're rolling along like a wheel. We're going so fast it's hard to tell which is which. In fact, were rolling along really like a wheel rolling downhill. We're also each getting wider and wider until it fills the whole path between the trees. Going downhill we gain so much momentum that even when there's an uphill the momentum carries us over that, effortlessly. There's just a change in the rhythm of it. We seem to be rolling down into deep valleys and up over high peaks now, exhulting in the acceleration as it builds toward the bottom and then the rise up the next slope . . . there is a beautiful precision, a beautiful delicacy in the sense of the diminishing acceleration, where it's just poised at the peak, very delicately, until we go into the next downhill run. He says most people are afraid of these extremes in acceleration.'

'But not you?'

'I have been also. He's showing me how thrilling it is. And also that I can't roll alone. It takes the two of us to form that wheel. His humour is much more in movement than it is in organization. It's like riding a roller coaster.

'I tell him that it feels like my brains are getting all jumbled, and he says, "That's good! Brains are like eggs, they're better when they're scrambled."

'We're going so fast now that we leave the path as its peak and go on up into the air and then back down. He makes the analogy between this and levitation. He indicates that to gain that levitation one really needs to flow full speed down into the valley. The valley's like a little pocket and there's just a beautiful fit there. He's also telling me something about levity, that if one is afraid of going down into the deep pockets then one can't gain the acceleration one needs in order to have some levity. So going down there is also an aspect of levity, it's closely connected with levity.

That I can be furious . . . like a clown . . . and that is being truly furious. But when I take my furiousness seriously, then I get stuck right in the gliding moments of levity. It's as if the path were paved with molasses, to take my furiousness seriously.'

'Is there more that you want to ask him about the Dean or the Chairman?'

'He shows me that they're stuck in their own molasses, and says for me to appreciate them doing that. To see the humour in it. He says that they're no different from me when I get stuck in my own molasses, when I take myself seriously. He says to live with levity does not mean *not* to deal fully, but it means to deal so fully that the facet of humour, of levity, is *also* there. And I've been leaving that out.'

'And does he have any suggestions for dealing with them fully?' I asked.

'His suggestion is to stay free and not get mired in their molasses. He's also showing me something else about levity. I had this view of a path as just being straight ahead and bounded by these great big trees, but at the peak of levitation one is really free, so the path is really the whole world rather than this narrow thing between the trees. It goes beyond them, kind of a rocket involved in space, like the space shuttle.

'There's an axis through the earth so that it always rolls along like a wheel. He tells me I've also been taking the earth too seriously. That it also has its humour. He shows me the earth laughing, enjoying itself, rolling along. He tells me I've taken the whole universe too seriously, and he shows me that the universe is also enjoying itself. It's almost like by not living in my own levity I have extricated myself from participating in the universe. And he's showing me that also in my research, I should do it very seriously but also with tongue in cheek, and see the humorous thread running through it. He says that humour is like breathing. You stop it and you die.

'He shows me also that our galaxy is like this wheel, just rolling along. And he takes me further out and shows me that the whole universe is like a wheel. He's indicating to me also that, first of all we both become very big and roll along just like the universe is doing, and then he shows me that all of mental illness involves taking something too seriously, involves tremendous loss of perspective. And that Norman Cousins is right in his sense of humour being so healing.

'He's showing me now that my whole body has been like a jaw, a very set jaw. And then he laughs, and tells me that the healthiest households are those that laugh. He tells me I've taken my life too seriously. He's showing me that my view of "being serious" means "without humour", and that maybe to really be serious is to always allow the facet of humour. To be serious is to be total. Not exclusive. He's showing me that my father took himself so seriously that he refused to allow humour, and that I bought his perspective, his idea of what seriousness is. And that my father mistook seriousness for his . . . that there was confusion in him between being serious and being angry.

'He tells me to remember that humour is health.' (At this point Raoul suddenly laughs uproariously.) 'He shows me a wheel where half of it is missing and it clunks along.'

'What is the other half?' I asked.

'He says the other half is everything else. He says a wheel without humour rolls, but the flat half, as it falls over and whams itself into the road, is constantly jarring. He seems to be indicating that to live without humour is to punish oneself. And he shows me Cantinflas with a halo on his head, like a saint.'

'It's time to leave so say goodbye for now.' (It was time for my next class.)

'He hugs me tightly and dives into my mouth. He keeps circling around like a fish within me.'

'Are you ready to leave now?'

'Yes. He wants me to take him with me.'

'Is that okay?'

'He's circling around inside my gut. It feels like we turn into a starfish or fireworks of some kind and shoot out in all directions, like a star trying to join the whole universe.'

8.

THE BABY KING

By now Raoul had become highly comfortable with the process of visualization. The speed with which his visualization developed surprised me, and I attributed it to his intense need to grow. He had developed a deep trust in me, and the range of his communication with me had broadened greatly.

One day he came to me and said he would like to do a visualization but that he had nothing in mind, no particular questions, nothing that he particularly needed to know on that occasion, and that he couldn't tell me *why* he wanted to do one![1]

He was already sitting in the recliner and I asked him to lie back, close his eyes, and take some deep breaths. I then asked him to imagine that he had roots growing from his body deep into the earth. Roots which both nurture and anchor.

He quickly replied, 'Yes, I feel the roots going deep into the earth. Now it feels like those roots are growing, they're branching out tremendously, to the point where they fill up the earth. The earth is like a round flower pot and the roots just fill it up. My whole source is the earth entirely, and this thing that is Raoul right here seems to be only on the crust.'

'Continue with that image and see where it goes,' I replied.

'It feels like the roots have grown only recently . . . many root fibres that are very alive and very moist. Also, when I inhale it feels like I am breathing in all of the space that exists.'

At this point Raoul took a deep breath, almost a sigh.

'My imagination is like a white flower, very clear, very uncluttered. Like a white petalled flower. Very firm petals that are almost waxy, like the leaves of a succulent plant, very full. Somewhat like the petals of a lotus blossom.

'In the centre of the flower is a little terrain, a little country, a little tiny country. I grow little and tiny myself and go explore.

'It looks like it's brown and barren, but as I get closer it's more like California country where the earth is yellowish and brown, but the trees are healthy and very green. There's a path that winds around and goes up to a castle. Right in the centre there is a white hill and the castle is built on top of the hill. It's made out of stones that are brown, like sandstone, and it seems to grow out of the earth. There is no firm delineation between the castle and the earth.

'I'm walking along the path now, which winds clockwise around the castle, and it brings me up to the door. There's a moat around the castle and a front gate which needs to be let down. But there's also a little door. I knock at the door.

'A strange creature on the other side lets me in. It looks like a mouse or a rat, but yet it has a bird's beak. It has fur and little hands, like a marmoset. It grasps things very quickly. It does seem to have some feathers coming out of its head. It's a strange looking creature with very well defined eyes. It can see very precisely and very quickly and takes in everything.

'I walk in as it opens the door and I say, "Hello, I'm not quite sure why I'm here."

'And it says, "That's okay. We know why you're here. Come in."

'I go in and realize that he just has to convey me to whoever it is that lives there, that's waiting for me. He's very friendly.' Raoul suddenly emitted a burst of laughter and then explained, 'I asked him what his name is and he says, "You can call me Sam Butler." He's just totally open. Just right there. He's very friendly, very cordial, very present.

'I feel right at home with him, like we're very old acquaintances. We chat as we walk along. It feels good to be with him.

'We're walking along an outer corridor. It's open to the sky. It's an open outer corridor that rings the castle on the inside. It's a nice day. As we get higher we can see the whole countryside out beyond the walls of the castle. It's quilted with different coloured fields.

'It feels like a medieval castle. But it also feels very cosy and I feel very at home here. We walk around the castle once on that parapet, counterclockwise. We come to a main entry into the bowels of the castle and I enter in.

'Inside it's very rich, really richly decorated, beautiful reds and blues and yellows. Remarkably colourful. I thought it would be very austere and it's not. It's just beautifully decorated, and richly done. There are stained glass windows around at strange angles which admit the light to particular places. Oriental rugs are spread on the floors, and colourful tapestries hang on the walls. It's very rich, very grand to be here. The colours are deep and engaging.

'Sam Butler is still with me, talking all the way. He talks more from a feeling place. This is a castle more to feel. It's a very deep place.

'The entry hall is long, remarkably long, and there's a king in a room which is right at the centre of the castle. And I can see a light, a very bright light, coming from the door. I have this image of a fat, jolly king inside, but I'm not really inside yet. It's just what I anticipated being in there once I get there. But the light is very bright, very intense. It comes from the double doorway that leads into the inner chamber. Sam and I get very close to it.

'The door is open, and as we step into it I see that the inner chamber goes all the way to the roof of the castle and is topped with a cupola which has windows around it, and they beam down very bright light at angles and it floods the room. The chamber itself is round.

'There are steps that go up. They are round platforms, one on top of another, which create a series of steps. On the top platform there seems to be a little baby under a bell jar, a glass covering. But I also have the image of that fat, jolly king. It seems to be my own image, that fat, jolly king, an image that I brought with me. So it's surprising to encounter this little baby that looks like it might be premature. And it's like it's in an incubator, but it's a bell jar.

'I ask Sam, "What's the meaning of this?" and he says that the baby is dead. And I say to him, "I don't understand." He tells me they have brought me here so I can breathe life into the baby. He then lifts off the top and I kneel down and breathe into the baby's mouth . . . like mouth to mouth resuscitation. The baby's cold, but it's not dried or deteriorated. It's as if it has not been alive . . .

'The baby lets out a deep cry that comes all the way from inside of it, totally. It's like a deep cry with no air in it. Or a cry that's been there for ages. It's gasping now for air, I continue to help it breathe by breathing into it and also by compressing its thorax. It's letting out these deep guttural cries. Like it's all sound and no air. It's as if the baby has been permitted no air until now. As if under the bell jar was a vacuum. And it's like the air is too coarse for it so that the air is raw in its throat. The air scrapes its throat.

'And it then settles down finally and starts breathing on its own. And it turns into a plump fat little baby. It's all swaddled up in very soft wool, very soft wool. It's fat and chubby.

'I hold him and I let him nurse at my breast. It's as if I can give him milk, and it just seems like a totally natural thing to do. And I hold him and we're just very close.

'It feels like I am to live there on top of those round platforms. I'm just supposed to live there and raise the baby. That's what is expected of me and that's what I expect to do. All my needs are taken care of when I'm there. Sam and the other . . . other . . . I don't know what to call them, other beings around there scurry around bringing me whatever I need. So it feels like I'm completely tended. Like my job there is to raise the child. Anything I want is there.

'I was kind of rocking the baby and then suddenly there's a big rocking chair, and I sit very comfortably in it. It fits my body. A really deep rocking chair that almost seems oversized. So I hold him there and rock. And he just kind of sleeps. He's very chubby and his skin is very pure, very alive, and he's very content.'

'Does he have a name?' I ask.'

'He's the King,' Raoul answered.

'Two words come when I ask that, one is Rex and the other is King. Kind of like the King is born. It's almost a contrast to the French saying, "The King is dead, long live the King." "The King is born. Long live the King."

'It feels like there is nothing to do, in fact nothing that I even desire to do but look at the baby, be here, take care of the King. And there's no hurry . . . and nothing particularly to do. Just stay close to the baby.

'Kind of like he grows at his own pace. It's also like there's a connection between him and me. It's not a visible connection but an energy connection which is also a guide to his growth . . . a channel by means of which he grows.'

Raoul was silent for a while. There is suddenly a surprised look on his face. I ask him, 'What's happening now?'

'It's as if I can experience the situation from the standpoint of the baby also, as well as from the standpoint of myself! It's like I'm very healthy, and I'm feeling really relaxed. And I'm swaddled up in a very soft fabric, and Raoul is here just to take care of me. It's his only task.'

'Do you need to tell him anything you need, or does he know?' I asked.

'No, he's very attentive, very aware, and it's as if he knows what I need. It's like I've been . . . like I have waited for him under that glass jar for a long time, many years that he took to get here. And now here he is, right on schedule. But I feel totally cared for, totally comfortable. It's like I have very little to do . . . just to feel good and grow, and that will take care of itself. There's nothing I need to do. It's all done for me.'

Raoul breathes deeply and stretches his arms. I asked him, 'What's happening now?' There is a long pause, during which he stretches intensely. Then he answers.

'It feels like my face is growing, taking on more of a defined character. Also it felt like there was a space in there where I'd gone through this before, and there was a sudden point at which everybody suddenly began demanding things of me: "Do this, do that, do the other." It was very bombarding. I was quite surprised. And it feels like there's nothing to do but grow, and that it should be a very enjoyable thing, something that feels very good . . . and I talk to . . . Raoul talks to Sam Butler about what should I do now, and Sam Butler says, "Don't do anything, just enjoy it, just be here."

'It's almost like from some distant place there comes a . . . mmm . . . an urgency to move, and yet, from this place . . . there's no need to move.'

Raoul stretches and yawns.

'It's also as if I can readily move from being the baby to being Raoul taking care of the baby and back to being the baby again . . . very free . . . free circuit there. And they both feel very good, really good, like it's just a joy that is right from the very core of my muscles. An enjoyment. It feels like when you have really exerted yourself physically, so much so that your muscles hurt, but n that hurting you really feel them good and deeply.'

R oul breathes deeply and openly.

'And I ask Sam Butler again, "What should I do now?"

'And he says, "Just enjoy."

'But it almost feels like for your sake I have to do something, but on the other hand there's nothing to do,' Raoul said to me.

'Yes. Just enjoy,' I replied.

Note:
1.   I was highly pleased at the fact that Raoul wished to do a visualization with no evident motive. In my experience this has indicated a new respect for a deeper, inarticulated source of motivation, and a trust in more central elements.

PART THREE

EXPLORING RELATIONSHIPS

What is relationship with another person? How can we live in harmony — growing and continuing to discover that magic fit, that blossoming which we call relationship? This section presents two examples of the use of visualization in resolving obstacles and enhancing an ongoing relationship.

9.

CLEARING THE AIR

She knocked at my office door. An edge of uncertainty in her eyes was quickly covered by her pretty smile. I had met her years before in the hospital where I was a nurse and she was a young mother with a dying husband. Her son, Jase, was only four then, and I was involved with listening and support for them both as they prepared for his father's death. It had been a slow and difficult process and Andrea and I had come to know each other well. We had maintained contact throughout the years that followed. I occasionally saw Jase, too. By now he was almost thirteen, slightly built and with a dreamy innocence that had not yet been lost to adolescence.

I asked Andrea in and she sat on the edge of the recliner. She had been very well, she said, and happy. She had met a man, Paul, six months ago and their relationship was blossoming into something warm and solid. There was only one problem. Paul and Jase did not get along. There were no arguments, really, just a cold lack of involvement. I asked her how she had been handling this and she explained that she merely tried to keep them separated. When involvement was necessary she behaved like a 'recreational director on board ship, dragging Jase and Paul from their deck chairs to a game of shuffleboard that neither wanted to play.'

I listened to her description and explained a little about visualization. I asked if she would like to look at her problem in this
way. She agreed.

I guided her through a fairly long relaxation exercise and then
the following visualization took place.

'I seem to be in a little clearing in a forest, and it's night time.
And there's a campfire there, and Paul and Jase and I are all sitting
around the campfire. And we're spaced absolutely equally around
the fire. So there's quite a distance between us. And the fire is
what attracts my attention. It's unusual in that it's . . . has
. . . some mass to it that is just red but it doesn't look like flames,
it's . . . I'm aware that the campfire is somehow my heart. It's
red and it's . . . the flames are coming off the sides of my heart.'

'Ask that campfire if it is your guide.'

'I ask, but I'm distracted by something down at the base of the
campfire. Like little sticks or ashes. Let me see.

'There are eyes in the darkness all around and I'm so distracted.
I . . . I ask the campfire if it's my guide . . . and then I'm so distracted
that I don't get an answer. It seems like what I'm going to do is
step back a little into the dark.'

'Before you do that see if there is a guide present that is in touch
with every element in the situation there: the fire, you, Jase, Paul
and all of those eyes.'

'All right. There seems to be a little stick at the base of the fire.'

'Ask that little stick if it is your guide.'

'He says that he is my guide and that I need to ask quickly
because he'll be gone.

[Crying] 'It's something about the giving, it's something about
allowing, it's something about . . . letting the . . . letting the fire
consume the little stick. He says that he'll be consumed and that
he will go into the air and be warmth.'

'Are you ready to let him be consumed?'

'He's ready . . . he's ready to let himself. He says . . . he says
that when he's consumed then the warmth will be everywhere
and that I can understand. And I still see the little stick but somehow I can see a little bit farther when the stick is consumed and
it feels like I can feel it inside and outside of everybody that's in
the clearing. I can see the warmth all around me. I feel I can see

the warmth inside of Jase and Paul and me. It's kind of like a pink glow.'

'Ask that warmth whatever you need to ask it.'

'I'm aware that we're all sitting and we're all a distance away from each other and I feel like asking the warmth how we can move closer together.

'The warmth seems to indicate I need to look at all of us separately. There's some kind of stupidity that I see with this huge fire and all trying to crowd to one side. There seems to be something I need to look at about everyone absorbing the warmth from their own spot.

'I . . . I'm paying attention to the eyes in the forest. And they're very alert eyes, they're almost dangerously alert.'

'See if you can watch the situation from their perspective.'

'Uh huh. One set of eyes that I see belongs to a large lion and he's in the forest but he's walking slowly around the clearing. He walks around and sees each person from the back. He sees Jase from the back. Jase's sitting kind of forward and he has his hand stretched out to the fire. And his head's bent. He's looking down at the ground.

'And then he sees me from the back. He can't really see how I look, he can't see who I'm looking at. I have my hands on the ground on either side of me.

'And then he walks around and sees Paul. Paul has his . . . he's holding his head in his hands and he's looking at the ground.

'It's almost like the lion is trying to decide who to pounce on. He's in no hurry.

'The whole . . . the whole circle's quite pink.'

'Let the lion go to each person there, starting with Paul, and see the situation from the perspective of how that person needs to grow.'

'All right.

'The lion goes to Paul and Paul turns and he stands and there's something about the . . . the pink warmth that keeps him from wrestling with the lion. The lion rears up on his hind feet and there's something about the pink warmth that keeps Paul from wrestling with the lion. It's too thick. It's like it's slow motion. The lion reaches out and Paul reaches out but they can't quite touch each other. It's like a dance. And the atmosphere just feels thick and stifling. Jase stays looking down, he doesn't see what's happening. It's like the warmth is some kind of buffer, but I can't tell if it's good or bad.'

'What does Paul need to do?'

'I think he needs to try wrestling with the lion and I don't know who would win.'

'What keeps him from wrestling with the lion?'

'What's keeping him now is that it's too pink in the clearing. The air is too thick and he reaches out and he can't quite touch the lion. He needs to go into the forest where the air is very cold and very clear and he could be very quick and alert.

'I'm watching and it seems like Jase needs to watch too, but he's not watching. He's just oblivious to what's happening, and the danger.'

'What does the lion need to tell you about Paul?'

[deep beathing] 'I'm not sure.'

'Allow the lion to leave Paul and move on to Jase.'

'The lion was . . . was dangerous with Paul, but with Jase he acts like he's a little cub. He's just playful and Jase suddenly becomes quite involved in playing with him and kinda teasing him. They're wrestling together. And Jase is just totally involved with . . . with playing with him.

'And Paul just sat back down and he's not watching. He's not watching Jase. He just sat back down and put his head in his hands.'

'Allow the lion to leave Jase and come to you.'

'All right.

'I'm with the lion and it's a mother lion and she came and sat down right next to me. She's sleek and gentle and she's just sitting real close to me. I feel her right next to me. We're both looking into the fire and we're just feeling each other's presence. We're not looking at each other. I ask her what she represents.

'And she says it doesn't quite make sense since she's a lion, but that she represents *Humanness.*'

'Ask her to tell you about your relationship to Jase and Paul.'

'She's looking at them both and just kind of shaking her head. She says they both have a lot to learn.'

'Ask her what they need to learn.'

'She says that Jase sees no relationship between the cub and the grown lion and that Paul sees no relationship between the grown lion and the cub. And that somehow I could . . . I could help them see the connection. Let me see if she can tell me how I could do that.'

'Ask her for specifics.'

'Uh huh. She's . . . she's standing up like she's going to use her claw to give me some advice. Maybe write in the sand, I'm not sure.

'The first word she writes is "task". I don't understand that.

' "Space" . . . the next word is "space". I feel distracted. I feel like I don't want to watch what she's writing.'

'What is she writing? Task, space . . . ?'

'Uh huh. "Giving." She wrote that. "Giving."

[long pause]

'My feeling now is that things are changed a little, and . . . I'm an Indian Chief sitting by the fire and I have a peace pipe and I'm trying to get both Jase and Paul interested in smoking it. And Jase is off playing with the lion cub and he doesn't even listen to me. And Paul's sitting there with his head in his hands and there's this huge male lion behind him and he's trying to ignore it, and he's not listening to me.

'And I'm sitting there. I have a blanket over my shoulders and I have long braids and a real wise face and I'm trying to get their attention.

'Suddenly I feel very powerful like what I can do is just reach out my hand and whatever I point to will levitate so I can make everybody change places. I can put Paul over next to the lion cub and he'll play and I can put Jase over by the grown lion. I can change everybody around.'

'Try it.'

'It's . . . [crying] it's very touching because I can see Paul like a little boy and he's so beautiful and so gentle, and he's playing, and he's happy.

'And I can see Jase and he's strong and he's brave, and he's all grown up, and he's not afraid. And the pink is all gone. And it seems like it's very clear.

'It's like they can see themselves in the way that I see them.'

'So somehow you can help them see that larger part of themselves?'

'Uh huh. I feel . . . I feel that feeling of . . . something about my heart. There's something about . . . let's see . . . there's something that's about the . . . about the pink warmth that's so oppressive. There's something about . . . there's some hopelessness in it like it's protective because the strength isn't there, but if I look and I see the strength then, if I see the strength in them, then I don't have to protect them. And the warmth is there when they come but it doesn't have to make them weaker, or interfere.

'I feel like I can see them and they both keep going from boy to man and back and forth and back and forth. Task, space, and giving. I think I understand it. My heart feels very big.

'It's an interesting picture. I feel ready to leave. But as I'm ready to leave I look at the whole picture and we're all still an equal distance around the campfire and the air is very very clear, and the lioness sits right next to me and I have a white blanket around me and white feathers, and everyone is absolutely clear with each other. I mean we look at each other and there's recognition, and there's contact, and there's some white about everyone. Paul's an Indian, too, and he has on a white loin cloth, and he's doing work. And Jase is a little boy again and there's something white about him, too. He's dressed just like Paul. And the campfire is a very manageable size.'

'Nothing feeding it that clouds the air?'

'No. And the forest isn't as . . . isn't as ominous. It's like it is depth. I see the depth but not the frightening feeling. I feel very . . . I feel very quiet, and I feel very strong.'

'You are.'

10.

THE DARK GUIDE

Vergil was thirty-two. He had grown up on a remote ranch in Montana. When he was twelve his parents had divorced and he had remained on the ranch with his father's bitterness while his mother and two sisters moved to Texas. In high school he was shy and withdrawn. During this time he developed an interest in reading which nurtured and enriched his lonely hours, but which also perpetuated his aloneness. It also led him to college and to a degree in Social Work.

In college he met and married a young woman who was also from a broken home and they lived a life which was superficial but which Vergil tended to idealize. And he was shocked and broken when she left him for another man. He compensated for his grief by devoting himself wholeheartedly to his job, which was in the children's division of a county welfare agency. His dedication soon earned him promotion to a supervisory position and it was in this capacity that he met Jerrine.

Jerrine was a caseworker in a nearby community and he met her at a state convention of social workers. There had been an immediate rapport between them and they began sitting together at the different sessions. During the final meeting before the convention ended, Vergil had opened up his heart to Jerrine and poured out the loneliness and isolation that he had carried for so long. He was also loquacious about his aspirations and his hopes for the future. She listened warmly and receptively, and then shared with him her own pain and vision. They found themselves deeply in love.

They saw each other as frequently as they could and soon found themselves engaged to be married. It was at this point that the conflicts began which ultimately brought Vergil to me.

It began one evening when he phoned her and she didn't answer. He called again everal times and still received no answer. He immediately began thinking she was out with another man. The next day when he finally reached her she told him she had been visiting an aunt. His suspicion did not diminish, however, and he began formulating a fantasy of her involvement with someone else and his eventual rejection. His suspicion of her unfaithfulness continued, even though on each occasion he would ultimately feel that she was not being deceptive, nor unfaithful.

As Vergil recounted his situated to me it was evident that two definite patterns persisted in his life, unfaithful women whose actions resulted in the dissolution of a relationship, and Vergil's tendency to retreat, to withdraw into isolation rather than endure the difficulties of relationship. In addition to other, more expressive modes of therapy, visualizations were also utilized. The following is one of them.

'Take a deep breath and allow your eyes to close. Feel the contact that your body makes with the recliner and the support that it gives you. Imagine that your body is growing roots that go deep into the earth, roots that provide nourishment and that also anchor you.

'As you become aware of the rhythm of your breathing imagine that each time you inhale you are taking in fresh energy, and feel that energy swirling around throughout your body, throughout your being. Imagine also that as you exhale you are getting rid of everything you no longer need, you are letting go of everything that is stale and dead, so that breathing becomes both beautifully renewing and deeply relaxing.

'Now allow there to be an openness in your imagination, a

cleared space, an emptiness where you can go in order to meet the guide who can tell you about your relationship with Jerrine. It may look like someplace you've been before, or it may look like no place you've ever even seen before, but wherever it is for you on this occasion, describe it to me when you begin to see it.'

'Yes, it's evening, things are dim and shady. I seem to be in a park, I can see trees and hedges around, and it's grassy, but there are some square objects that I can't quite make out. They seem to be made of stone. There's something there that feels like a tomb, very cold and marble grey.

'There's a stairway that goes down . . . into a crypt. I'm going down it. Something strangely foreboding about it but yet it's not scary. Looks like it's very dark down in there. Now I notice that there are torches on the walls, like in an old medieval castle. It feels like an old medieval castle where I'm going way down deep into the dungeon. It's a long, long way down. The stairs are stone, the walls are stone, the ceiling is slightly arched.'

'Are you alone?'

'Yes, I'm alone. No. there seems to be something hovering along with me, more like an apparition, a ghost, robed in grey, just floating along behind me and slightly to the left. I turn around and it has a skull for a face, skeleton hands, no feet. It just kind of floats along.'

'Ask it if it is your guide.'

'I ask it if it is my guide and it says, "No, I am your death." And it tells me that it is always with me wherever I go. And I ask it why I can see it on this occasion and it says that we're going to a place where I will be very close to my death.'

'Ask it what it's name is.'

'I ask it and it chuckles and says it doesn't need a name. I'm not afraid of it at all. In fact, it feels kind of cosy down in here.

'It feels like we've arrived at a landing and there's a doorway. There's a slight turn in the passageway just about 20 degrees to the right through the doorway and down a few more steps. It's dark in there, kind of eerie, so that you don't . . . you just have a fuzzy sense of the dimensions of the walls. And I don't really know what I'm supposed to do there.'

'Ask if your guide is there, the guide to your relationship with Jerrine.'

'I ask if my guide is there and there's no answer. It's very dark.

'It's hard to see and so I realize that what I need to do down there is just to feel, feel the place, not see it. It's like my body has become a radar system. And as I feel the place I realize that my sensitivity fills up the chamber.

'It's a fair-sized room. The ceiling is higher than that of the passageway through which we came. The walls are stone but there's a fuzziness to them, feelingwise. From the perspective of feeling it's almost like the room is upholstered in dark velvet, although from a visual standpoint the walls would be stone and mortar. And a voice says, "Now I am here for you."

'The voice says, "I am not the kind of guide you can see." It says, "But you can feel me, and we will communicate through your feeling."

'I tell it that it's vital that I understand my relationship with Jerrine. And it shows me a deep, long tunnel. Not in vision, but in feeling. Full of mystery, and endless. And it tells me that the tunnel is analogous to my relationship with Jerrine.

'The voice tells me that at the convention I came to the point of caring about her from my being, from my heart. Not in terms of what she did, but just caring. With no qualifications. And it tells me that my intellect goes wild trying to impose qualifications because that was so hideously done to me when I was very young. And it tells me that the qualifications imposed on me were not consistent, and so I could never have any firm sense of them, and therefore never conformed to them. So that my own boundaries always remained kind of an undefined mystery, and that that was my great gift. If they had been consistent, I would have defined myself and lived in terms of that definition. Since they were so fuzzy and undefined I could not really grasp who I was, and therefore the mystery of who I was was constantly present, even though very threatening, very terrifying, at that time when I was still growing. It tells me that I struggled to have an identity, and that I would put on whatever identity I thought someone else wanted of me at that time, but then I could just as easily take it off. So I felt always unfixed, always unsettled, but it was only because I was trying to fix myself. If I had accepted my fluidity I would have been really centred. I was always trying to fix myself into a static position. Whereas lack of fixedness constantly pointed me back in the direction of my fluidity.

'It tells me that as soon as I find something fixed in my relationship with Jerrine, then I will just as soon find something unfixed. And I ask, "Well, what about her welfare in this?" And it says, "The way you can help her grow most is just to love her, without qualifications." It says, "That is where your own growth will come from also."

'He's coming and doing something to my heart. It feels like my heart has been encased in tin, and he's cutting open the tin container, and opens up the tin which forms very sharp, dagger-like edges, and then he rolls them back so that they can't cut. He asks me if I want to do it all now and I say yes. He says, "This is for your own growth."

'And he keeps rolling those cut pieces back, clear around to the back of my heart, and at the back of my heart they become very small but very concentrated. And then they enter right into the inside of my heart, and become like fluid silver, like quick-silver, inside of my heart. My heart feels very unprotected now, and I hadn't realized how protected it was. I was very insensitive to it. And it's like that quicksilver is now inside of my heart, totally shapeless but very brilliant. It's totally fluid and just very fast, just like quicksilver. Lightning fast.

'And he tells me that I have tried to limit my love for people because some of them hurt me. But that if I limit my love for them then I just perpetuate the hurt that they initiated. He tells me that I need to love people, but not arrogantly. To love them as if they were just now evolving. As if they were just now waking up. And as if in their sleep and blindness they have done many things which have hurt others. And that I need to help them awaken very gently.

'He says that in defending ourselves . . . in people defending themselves, they do hurt others. But what they're really trying to do is just protect themselves. But they have mistaken defence for protection. He says that defence only diminishes a person, diminishes their awareness, because it blocks out the world; originally they can see, and then they form a shell through which they can no longer see. He tells me that my suspiciousness is my shell. And that it is just misguided awareness. And that if I will just love people without qualification, then I will be very aware.

'He says that as soon as I become accusatory then my awareness closes down. He says, "You can't hurt by loving." He says, "Loving is each person's greatest gift, something they can enter into completely voluntarily. The difficulty is that they try to make other people responsible for their loving. They refuse to own that responsibility themselves." He tells me just to love Jerrine and she will be true to me in the best way she can, and if I try to force her being true, then that will limit her. Her being true to me needs to be voluntary in order for it to have any sense of quality. If I try to force her to be true I diminish her spark.

'And then I ask him what about me? And he says, "Ahhhh, don't try to define yourself. Appreciate the mystery. You've been given a great gift. There's been much misery through which you've had to see your way clear. But that has just shown you the route of your growth. You've felt miserable only because you couldn't see the growing that was going on. Stay fully immersed in your mystery and appreciative of it."

'I ask him what should I do about my suspiciousness, and he says, "Just love, without qualifications." He says, "Suspiciousness is an attempt to impose restrictions on your love, on your loving."

'I ask him what should I do to continue growing, and he says, "Enjoy your being. Don't get wrapped up in moroseness." He says, "Some of your path has been miserable. Don't think that your entire path, your whole path, has to be that way." He says, "Enjoy . . . the bird singing . . . the deer running . . . the snow falling . . . or the blossoms in spring . . . or a newborn baby."

'He says, "Come see me again whenever you need to. I'm always here." And then it feels like the chamber is filled with light and I can see the cold stone and mortar, and that is one level. But the level of feeling is also still present. The light is so bright that I tend to be drawn by that and lose sight of the deeper feeling, but it is always present. It seems to have a much deeper intelligence, a much more extensive . . . a much deeper perception than the realm of light. And I have the understanding that the realm of light is something that may allow a fine tuning of that deeper realm. But they're not supposed to be in opposition. The realm of light is like the icing on the cake. They're not opposed. But we get so involved with the icing that we loose sight of the cake. Icing enhances the cake. Yet to have only icing is no good at all.

There's no substance to it. You *can* have a cake with no icing but the icing *does* add to the cake. Decorates it, enhances its flavour, spices it. And the two need to be unified.

'I say to him, "Thank you," and he replies, "You're welcome." My death is still there over my left shoulder, behind me. And he feels very warm, almost alive, he's kind of chuckling. And I feel very much the wholeness that he brings to life. The fullness that he brings to life. He lets us see life much more fully, much more appreciatively, than if he were not present. Somehow he's like the icing on the cake. I feel a really deep, warm appreciation for my guide and for my death and for this chamber. Kind of like here I've learned to see in the dark.

'We make our way up the steps, me and Death. Me and *my* death. And outside it's beautifully sunshiny. We get up out of it and there are a lot of birds singing. And the trees have new leaves on them, very tiny still. And blossoms. And the air is rich and the sun is brilliantly warm. And I turn to my death and say goodbye. He puts his hands on my shoulder and says, "I'm always with you." '

PART FOUR

OVERVIEWING THE SELF

Freud's major contribution to our understanding of the human mind was his discovery and exploration of the realm he called the Unconscious. In the patients with whom he originated his theory and his therapy, he discovered elements which had broken forth and intruded into the Conscious (as in obsessives), or elements which needed to be conscious for the full functionability of the individual, and yet were not (the repressed). Much of the material also came from himself.

As with any theory, his own psychological dynamics illuminated the world he was describing: that is, he was biased. The unfortunate thing about this was the particular view of the Unconscious that he provided. He had a horror of the Unconscious, and he viewed it as horrible. One of his metaphors was of a basement in a house. The door to the basement was locked, but from it we can hear strange animal sounds and eerie noises. We try to strengthen the door and make sure it is bolted in order to keep whatever is down there from breaking up into the house. The Unconscious was scary.

This division was later refined into a division between the Ego and the Id, but the same conflict and struggle inhered in this new formulation. The Id is instinctive and animalistic and its energy must be captured by the Ego and channelled into effective or socially allowable actions. Essentially, the Ego needs to wrest control from the Id if a person is to be psychologically healthy. Unfortunately, this is a view *from* Ego, and Ego is plagued with limited perspective.

From our own experience and theoretical perspective the Unconscious is *not* fearsome, nor is it against life, culture, or the individual. It is, however, against repressive society, the forced domination of one person by another. And even here, it tries to placate and to find peaceful solutions before it resorts to open battle. And it *is* alive; vitally, profoundly, thoroughly alive.

The seeming opposition between the two arises because the Ego is not fully alive, but repetitive. Its trigger is similarities, and its action is similar to an action that has occurred in the past.

We have never found any element within an individual which is against the individual. We *have* found situations where some behaviour, thought, or attitude was utilized at one time because it was needed for apparent survival, and which still functions defensively even though the circumstances have since changed. It is like an obedient servant who was at one time given firm instructions as to his duties, and whose instructions have never been changed even though the situation in which those instructions were meangingful no longer exists, but he dutifully continues to do as he was originally instructed. From the territorial perspective we could say that a defence system was established, became ritualized, and continues to persevere, now to the *detriment* of the whole person, rather than contributing to his survival. Defence systems keep us in the past, but to be fully grown we need to be completely in the present.

These 'servants' are totally willing to change their tactics, but they have never been instructed to do so. Most of us live in a house with numerous preprogrammed servants whose duty was defence and protection, but who now form a battalion that does not let us go anywhere without them. Our venturing is tremendously hampered. And when they encounter anything that even resembles their preprogrammed enemy, they go into action. And one of their preprogrammed enemies is the Unknown.

The human problem is that our survival mechanism has constituted itself, over a period of time, and in bits and pieces, into a frozen structure which feels that its activity is the only thing that ensures our survival. The truth is that *its* activity is the only thing that constitutes *its* survival. The problem is that we have identified with the mechanism. We have confused the two: the survival of the defensive mechanism with the survival of the individual.

To relax the activity of the defence system means that we must be willing to encounter our fear. To move from identification with our defence system to identification with our greater totality, we must traverse our fear. But it is fear that triggers the defence system. How can we get out of this bind?

There are several ways out. One is to willingly encounter fear without resistance. Since the defence system is constituted of fear, avoidance and escape from fear, its perpetuation is automatically reinforced by that escape or avoidance. We must be willing to experience fear without this reinforcement. We must go directly into our fear rather than away from it. This does not mean that we must deliberately put ourselves in frightening situations. It means that when fear is present we must be willing to experience it rather than to turn it off in some way.

A second method is to gain an overview of the entire being that we are. Since our overviewing is also part of that being, this can only be accomplished metaphorically. We must develop the capacity of seeing beyond Ego, of seeing the full picture. Our strong identification with the defence system makes this difficult since it views everything outside itself as threatening (just as Freud viewed the Unconscious). We have found that deep visualizations reflect that larger perspective, and themselves constitute a movement toward growth and integration.

It is probably this movement toward growth that saves any of us. There is a deep level at which we know whether growth is being enhanced or diminished. The only thing worthy of an intelligent culture is to invest itself fully in whatever is growth-enhancing. Only then can we bring our maturity and wisdom to full fruition.

We can also develop an orientation of utilizing every situation in our lives for growing, and trusting that deep directionality. This is certainly a good first step: to ask of every situation, no matter how difficult it may seem, 'How can I grow from this?' This provides a new perspective for our defensive Ego, one which gradually builds a new connection out of the short circuit that is the defensive Ego.

The following four visualizations, all from the same young mother, illustrate the capacity of deep visualization to provide an overview and initiate an integration between the defensive Ego and that larger realm of aliveness and fulfilment which is our natural heritage.

11.

INA AND THE TIGER

'As you relax deeply, allow there to be a space, an openness in your imagination, a clearing. And in that clearing allow there to begin to emerge the place where you need to be in order to meet today's guide, in order to do today's work, where you can meet a guide who can tell you what needs to be done now, what way you need to grow now. Don't try to push it or force it. Don't even try. Just allow. And when that place emerges, tell me what it's like.

'Where are you now?'

'There's a very steep cliff, like . . . a . . . um . . . I'm not sure it's the ocean but a big body of water I can't see across, and I'm on top of a very steep cliff that goes directly down to the water. There are gnarly kinds of trees at the top that seem to be clinging to the edge. And I can't really see myself there, it almost feels like I'm one of the trees.'

'Uh huh. Allow yourself to be one of the trees. What does it feel like?'

'It feels like I have to hang on very tightly, it's very windy and . . . I have the feeling of having to crouch very low, close to the ground.'

'Is your guide anywhere?'

'I see a kite. It's pink. I can't see who's holding the string, but on up the cliff I can just see a kite flying in the wind.'

'Call to the kite. Ask it if it is your guide.'

'It doesn't answer. It seems very playful. Like it's just swooping and turning circles and going higher and lower and it's got a long tail. It's white. The tail's white. Made out of just a piece of cloth. Big bows. Big bows on its tail. Let me ask again.

'I . . . it feels like there's no way to communicate. It feels like I am stuck clinging to this cliff and the kite just keeps going in and out of my vision. Let me see what to do.

'I have a heavy feeling in my chest. I feel there's no way I can check out the kite because I'm rooted quite deeply here on the edge of the cliff. I'm where I can't see very far. I can see down into the water but the terrain is hilly and I can't see anything.

'I feel the kite ridiculing the scrubby tree, taunting it. I also feel how insubstantial the kite is. It would just take a little break in the string and it's gone.'

'Let the kite's string be tied to the tree so that the tree anchors it.'

'They seem completely incompatible. The tree allows the kite to be tied to a gnarly branch, but . . . I want to get a better feeling about what the tree thinks. The tree's not really a tree, it's more like a low bush, just a gnarly low bush. It sees no value in the kite. It allows it to be tied to one of its gnarly branches but it sees the kite as frivolous and it wouldn't care if it just blew away . . . And the kite wouldn't mind blowing away.'

'Allow it to blow away and see what happens.'

'It just floats up in the clouds. I don't want to let it go. There's no direction; it just goes up and down and turns in a circle. There's some kind of light feeling. Not a good feeling, a directionless feeling.'

'What does the kite need?'

'The kite needs someone to hang on to its string.'

'Who can do that?'

'I immediately picture some kind of male . . . male child who would take charge. It would go out with the purpose of flying the kite, and fly the kite, and run and play, and pull the kite in when it was done.'

'Would the kite enjoy it?'

'It would be glad for it. It feels like maybe it could feel the difference in the flight if . . . if it had familiar hands on the string. Now it's just floating the way the wind blows. I think I'll just do that.

'I can feel it but I . . . I'm getting confused about . . . I was feeling like a young boy was holding the kite, and I was feeling like he didn't quite seem reliable.'

'What would happen if you held the kite?'

'It feels like if I held the kite then I'd push other people away. I'd say, "Listen, I can do this."'

'Try it and see.'

'Now I'm standing there flying the kite. There's some kind of bitterness about it. It's not fun.'

'What needs to be there to make it fun?'

'All I see is this little boy and me. I'm holding on to the kite and I can do it very well. But . . . I'm not sharing it at all, and . . . I'm not liking this whole thing. I'm not sure, but it feels like I'm not allowing something.'

'What is it you're not allowing?'

'It seems like . . . everything in my landscape is very stark. It's like this child and I are standing on flat sand and it feels like what I need to allow is . . . a lot of greenery and life . . . I need to allow other people in there . . . let me see.

'I have this image of myself with a lot of children there and me taking all their kites and holding on to them because I don't trust them to fly the kites alone. There's . . . not a good feeling. I'm really confused with what I'm doing. I'm going to give the kites back to all the children and then walk away.

'I walk a little ways away. I'm standing on a rock and the children are watching. I get a strange feeling inside of my nose and in the bones right above my eyes.'

'Let that feeling do whatever it needs to do.'

'I have an image of an old lady who . . . goes round smelling things that are distasteful, kind of smelling bad smells. And I think it's me.'

'Why does she limit herself to bad smells?'

'I think she . . . I'll talk to her about it. She's not exactly me; I think she's my guide. She's an old maid. She has on a black dress . . . and is very proper looking. She has a very disdainful way of holding her head so she can sniff out evil and corruption and things that aren't very proper.

'She's sitting on a porch swing. I'm down on the sidewalk, sitting on the bottom step, just sitting there.

'She's having tea in some china cups but she doesn't offer me any. It looks like she wouldn't let anyone touch her things because they might break them. Everything about her house is absolutely immaculate. The house is white. The swing doesn't even creak when she swings and she's drinking tea out of her china cup. She says her name is Ina.

'I ask her if she's my guide and she says yes, she's going to show me how to live a proper life. I tell her that nothing about her seems to have any meaning. And she says you have to *assign* the meaning. I don't know what she means.'

'Ask her what she means.'

'She says you have to be in control. If you believe something's important it becomes important. It just seems like she's putting on some kind of an act for me.'

'Ask her about it.'

'She just acts more disdainful and ridiculous. I feel compelled to tell her that I think her life has no meaning, that nothing she values is important. It doesn't seem to faze her at all. It feels like nothing I could tell her would have any impact at all, like she would just go on drinking the tea, being ridiculous until she dies.'

'Ask her what that has to do with *your* life, what you need to learn about your life.'

'I ask her and she says . . . she says to me, "You are the one who is sitting on the porch swing." '

'Do you understand?'

'I understand her. I know what she says, but . . .'

'Ask her if she can give more clarification.'

'I can't seem to phrase the question but I keep trying. I ask her, "What does it mean to be on a porch swing?" and she says, "You go back and forth and back and forth and you always return to the same place." I don't understand that either.'

'Ask her if she can give you an example.'

'She shows me myself as a young girl sitting in a swing swinging back and forth, and there's something about . . . if I get off then I'll be old and I'll be wise. And I'm afraid.'

'I feel like my . . . like my body just aches. I feel like I've been in one position for so long. I feel like I need to get off, get off the swing and stretch. I don't know what it means, but . . .'

'Try it and see.'

'There's just nothing. I don't know, I stand up and stretch and there's nothing. I just feel nothing. It feels like I just stand up and walk around the porch, walk downstairs, walk in the grass . . . nothing, there's nothing different. It's not fearful . . . I just feel lost.'

'Tell Ina that you feel lost.'

'She feels just totally absent from me. She's there but she's ignoring me, I can't get her attention. I don't know. I'll try it again. She seems to be real scolding. She just leans back now. I sit on the porch floor beside her swing. I don't like her very much. I don't feel like being here.'

'Tell her that.'

'She said she didn't ask for me. She said I can go anytime.'

'Tell her you don't understand her guidance.'

'She says it's my choice.'

'I'm just . . . I'm just at a loss. It feels like all the . . . all the energy is in a circle around this . . . around this scene, and it just feels like I'm so stuck, it feels like I don't want to be here with Ina and how she lives her life. I'm just sitting here on the floor of the porch watching her swing and it feels like I would just go on like that forever and not move and just watch.'

'Feel that feeling of being stuck. Feel it to its very core.'

'I feel like I get up and walk around in the grass but I always come back and sit on the steps, or sit on the floor and just watch her swing, and nothing, it doesn't matter at all. Nothing matters at all.'

'Feel the feeling of being stuck. Feel it to its very core. Let it go all the way through. As if you were a magnifying glass, really see it totally, completely, for the very first time, feel it through in its entirety. Feel it so totally that it dissolves of its own accord. Feel it as if your awareness is a magnifying glass that burns through the stuck place. Feel it totally.'

[Much deep breathing]

'It feels like . . . like I'm looking at the scene from a long ways off. Like it's in a little tiny circle and I see Ina on the porch swing,

and I see myself sitting on the floor, and . . . I don't feel like I'm
out of being stuck but I feel like I can see a little better. Almost
like it's in a little bubble. I can see a much bigger world around it.'

'What is the world around like?'

'It's . . . it's kind of older, and . . . green. It's all overgrown
with trees. It's like the bubble is black and white, and the world
around is green and . . . and very alive.'

'See if there's a guide for you in that live part.'

'There's a tiger. I ask him what I should do about being trapped
in the bubble, and he says that when I'm ready all I need to do
is ask him and he will just go over and with one claw break the
bubble. And it'll be very easy.'

'What's his name?'

'He's snarling around and is so busy I can't get his attention.
It feels like I'm . . . I'm still in the bubble but I've come out of
the bubble to talk to the tiger . . . but I'm kind of black and white
for him and it's hard for me to get his attention because he's so
busy . . . and he's so full of life, it's like a shadow asking a question.
I can't get his . . . attention to ask his name. It feels like he would
tell me if he could . . . if he could see me, but he's too busy.'

'What do you need to do?'

'It feels like . . . it feels like I'm not ready to get his attention.
It feels like it's almost enough just to . . . to watch him. He's pretty
magnificent. He's doing all kinds of things. There are some huge
. . . bees, and he's allowing them to land on his nose and he's
. . . jumping around and brushing them off, but he's playing, and
he's rolling around . . . he's just a little too busy to interact with
but he's a lot of fun to watch. He's stretching and he's snarling
and he's rolling.

'You know, I think it's enough . . . it feels like it's enough to
leave with the picture I have. It feels like I'd like to go back to
visit the tiger another time.'

'Ask him how you might prepare, how you might get ready
for the bursting of the bubble.'

'All right. His answer is to breathe more colour into my life.
I think I know what he means. I can't explain it but I know what
he means.

'And my bubble is shrinking, shrinking, shrinking. This image
of myself with him is I'm very thin, and I'm black and white, but

I'm getting . . . taller, and I feel glad that he answered my question.
I feel like I'm done. I think I'll come back another time.'

12.

IVAN AND THE WARRIOR

'. . . and allow there to be a space, an opening, a place where you can go to do today's work. A place where you can learn about the relationship between your true self and your body.'

'I am on a country road. It is really little more than a path. It is wide enough for cars to travel but so few cars have come this way that grass has grown up between the tyre tracks. It has steep banks like the road is almost underground with the banks extending up on both sides, three feet maybe on one side and higher on the other side. The banks are overgrown with that kind of wild rose that opens up very wide. It is a curving road and I'm walking along it. I seem to be very young, like thirteen. I am all alone. I see no guide. But I feel like I will follow this path. It's very hilly. There are grasshoppers that are jumping in front of me from bank to bank. Some of them are sticky and they land on my skin. I don't mind them, really, I just brush them off.'

'What kind of day is it?'

'It's sunny. The sky is really blue and there are little white clouds. It's a warm day. I'm barefooted. The ground is soft and fine and it's dusty when I walk. There are clouds of dust behind me. I don't seem to be heading anywhere. I seem to be just ambling. There are some people off the road on a bank near some trees. I think they are loggers. I feel like not disturbing them, just noticing them and going on.

'There's a bluejay in a tree. I ask him if he's my guide and he says, "No" and flies off. There's a young child in a swing, a boy. I ask him if he's my guide and he says, "No". I have a sense of being way up above the scene, like where the clouds are, and I'm watching myself as I walk along the path. And the path just stretches forever and ever and ever. It just winds and winds. It looks like if I stay on it . . . there aren't any turn offs. I can't even see where it ends. It's not a bad path. There are things to see. But there is nobody to interact with. It's just a pretty path. I feel like telling myself to scramble up the bank and get off the path. I guess I'll do that.

'I argue with myself a little bit. The only way to get off the path is through all those roses. And I'm barefooted. It seems like it's a little too uncomfortable. It's steep. I'll just have to hang on to the vines and climb up through there. There doesn't seem to be one better place or another. It's just all difficult. My sense is to do the steep side, too, not the side that's not so steep. It's quite steep where I am, but I decide to do it. I'm hanging on to the vines and digging my toes into the dirt. I'm getting scratched up.

'The landscape's kind of bleak up above. Old dead corn stalks and fields that have been burned, fences that are in poor repair. And there is no path, just fields.'

'Can you find your guide?'

'There seems to be an old farmhouse. I'll go there and ask. It's in bad repair, too. It's tumble-down. The porch is just kind of caved in. There's a well. I'm having a hard time getting there for some reason. I'm repelled by it. I don't want to go there. A dwarf lives there. A deformed dwarf. It is dirty there.'

'Is the dwarf your guide?'

'I think so. He has just come out of the house. He's pumping water from the well. It's hard for him to do. I go close enough to ask him his name . . . Ivan is his name. I tell him that I have come to ask him about the relationship between my true self and my body. He tells me to sit down. I sit on the ground next to the well. He continues to pump water. I don't know the questions that I want to ask him. I feel like I want to ask him how he gets along there. It must be very hard for him. That question doesn't seem right to me. I think I'll sit here quietly on the ground and see if I can ask a question that I can make some sense of. He's jumping up and down. He's doing a dance, with canes to support him. And I sit there on the ground and he's jumping around.'

'Tell him that you're having trouble formulating the questions.'

'He says I should watch him. I watch and he changes as he dances. He is all stooped over, dancing with the aid of two canes, and then his form changes and he is straight and very big. He looks strong. He looks like an Indian warrior. He's very muscular and very quiet. The little dwarf is all stooped over and is wearing rags. And the warrior just emerges out of him until he's standing straight and tall wearing almost nothing. His skin is brown and he's very strong. I don't know what this means. It might mean that I'm everything, the dwarf and the warrior and the stages in between.'

'Which is your body and which is your true self?'

'I can't seem to get it right . . . the dwarf says . . . I can't quite get it. Something about pain. Seeing pain. With the dwarf it's expected, but no one can see the warrior's pain. I can see them both at the same time. When the warrior is here I can see the dwarf inside the warrior. But when the dwarf is here I can't see the warrior inside the dwarf.'

'Ask the dwarf which is your true self and which is your body?'

'. . . The dwarf says he is the true self. And he is inside the warrior. He's always there. And I can see him there. Others may not see him but it is obvious that he's there. The warrior is walking around. I am looking at the dwarf. He is curled up inside the warrior, kind of down in his abdomen. He's just curled up in there while the warrior is walking around. I can see him walking but I can't hear what he's saying.

'It is hard to understand. It is the warrior that talks. He says, "It is necessary to understand pain and to understand hurt to carry Ivan around inside of me." I get some images. They aren't in words but more feelings. I can see how it feels for the dwarf to be carried around inside the warrior and how it feels for the dwarf to be out and exposed. And have movement hard for him. How it feels for the dwarf to be inside the warrior and be carried everywhere and not have to feel the pain of every movement. It's like he can go everywhere and not have to feel the pain of every movement but nobody sees him. When he's inside the warrior nobody sees him. And if he's outside . . . it's like my feeling when I walked up to the farmhouse. I felt sorry for him. So he has a choice, of being out there on his own, being vulnerable and having life hard, or riding around inside the warrior and not letting anybody see him. I don't quite understand the meaning for me but that's what he feels. And so he chooses both ways. He chooses to live alone in this old dilapidated farmhouse and take care of himself and he also chooses to live inside the warrior and look out at the world from a strong place. I don't know what meaning this has for me but that's what it has for him. And there's not a judgement about it. He can do both things.

'I am confused about who to talk to. The dwarf says he hears no matter who I talk to. The warrior says he pays better attention if I talk to him, but he also hears if I talk to the dwarf. I feel like if I talk to the warrior the words come through his ears and drop down to the dwarf, but if I talk to the dwarf the warrior might be looking away and not hear. So I will talk to the warrior.

'The warrior says that it would be doing the dwarf a disservice to make himself less strong because if he is strong he can carry the dwarf around to see the world. He would be doing himself and the dwarf a disservice by being less strong. My feeling at first was that the dwarf resented the warrior but my feeling has changed. It's like the dwarf wants to be alone, to feel the way it's hard but he welcomes the warrior's strength.'

'Ask the dwarf if he has abilities that the warrior has not.'

'He says that he does. He says that he is the sensitivity and that he is . . . the part that feels . . . and the part that hurts . . .' [crying]

'Anything else?'

'And the part that struggles and the part that's real and . . . I feel like I understand it.'

'Ask the dwarf if there is some way that you can help him grow to his full stature.'

'He says by working and being alone. He says by allowing "the muscles to be sore", by allowing time. I have an image of the dwarf inside the warrior but he is standing up tall, and I have a sense that it could be that way.'

'Ask the dwarf what has caused him to be so dwarfed. What

has kept him from achieving his full stature?'

'The first thing he says is that he thought that was what was expected.'

'Who expected it?'

'Everyone expected it. That's the only answer I see.'

'Ask him if there is any way you can help him grow right now.'

'He says to come see him often. [crying] When I first saw him he looked very ugly. And when I see him now he is very beautiful. And he gives me a glass of water. I feel like I have a lot to learn from him. I look at the glass of water and I drink it. [crying] I feel ready to go. The dwarf hugs me goodbye and the warrior nods his head to acknowledge my going. I'll come back. The dwarf needs to fill the inside of the warrior so the skin's the same.'

13.

WREN AND THORNE

'I bend down to crawl through the flaps of a tent. The area inside is very flat, with short even grass growing for as far as I can see. The grass is not lush but it covers the ground.

'I see a maypole standing in the middle of this expanse. It has streamers coming from it that are pink and yellow and blue. The post is a very sturdy, substantial one but it is broken part way through about a foot from the bottom. It sways by itself from this broken place. If people were to hold on to the ribbons it would bend in the direction of whoever was pulling the hardest. But there are no people. The maypole is standing alone in this flat field of grass. I walk toward the pole and ask if it is my guide. It does not speak at first but moves clumsily from its break. I ask again. It says, "I will show you."

'Some little white animals appear. They are vague at first but then I see them clearly. They are small and white. They are stuffed animals. They are toys. I ask if they are my guides. They say, "Watch a little while." They are various little stuffed animals: a rabbit, a mouse, and a teddy bear. They are all white and very small. I watch as they each pick up a ribbon and begin to move in the under and over motion of the maypole dance. They weave

in and out and move around the pole. It is a joyless scene. They
are going through the motions. I move a distance away and
continue to watch. It seems such a lifeless dance. The ribbons
winding and unwinding. The repetition of the movements. Everyone repeats and repeats the going over and coming under.
Everyone is regimented and stuck.

'I'm aware that in moving away from the maypole I am now
standing under a tree. It's a big tree. A hawthorn tree. It is gnarly
and old and has many thorns. There is a bird in the tree. She is
building a nest. I can't see her clearly yet, but she is brown and
has some white strips. I ask her if she is my guide. She is too busy
to answer me. She is busy pulling the ribbons from the maypole
to make her nest. She goes to the maypole, flies to the top, pulls
one ribbon free and flies to her nest with it. When the ribbon is
pulled free the small animal rolls backward into the dust, flails
a few seconds, and stays where it has fallen, unable to move.

'She is destroying the maypole. It is strange that this destruction
makes me feel so bad. She says something to me. I only understand the word "illusion". I ask again. The word I hear this time
is "useful". I still don't understand so she stops a moment to speak
clearly to me. She says, "The maypole was an illusion of happiness
and it wasn't even a good illusion. I can use these coloured ribbons
in a useful way to make a nest for live baby birds." I understand
her words and I continue to watch her.

'She's kind of a funny bird. I've never seen a bird like her before.
You wouldn't say that she's beautiful. She's small and brown and
the stripes on her body run the length of her, from head to toe.
The stripes are a whitish grey. She is very busy. And suddenly
she has all the ribbons off the pole. All that is left in the distance
is the pole tipping off to the right and the little lifeless animals
lying in broken positions in the dust. I feel very sad.

'I ask the pole what I need to learn about destruction and my
relationships with children. He does not answer but the bird flies
to the pole and perches on the top. I ask her the same question.
She says she will take me on a journey. Suddenly I am very small,
or she is very big, because she can pick me up in her claws. She
flies very easily with me and in moments we are high above the
maypole. I see clearly the broken pole far below and the very
colourful nest made of ribbons. I see more clearly from this

distance and recognize the tree as a chinaberry tree rather than a hawthorn. We fly away from the scene until I can no longer see the big bright nest or the tree.

'We're flying so fast that the landscape below is unclear. There seems to be a canyon. We are so high in the sky. It occurs to me that she could drop me but the fear seems unfounded and I relax a bit more and allow myself to be carried along. She is strong and she is flying with purpose. I see a tiny river. I see fields. Cornfields. And a barn.

'It seems to be in my control where we land. And it seems that it is very hard to choose. I tell the bird that it is too hard for me to choose and she says that she will aid me. She says that she will take me to some guides if I will allow it. She says that I can call her "Wren". She is getting very tired. We have flown a long way. We are flying now toward the sun in a child's painting. The landscape is bright and everything has a heavy outline as if it was done with crayons. There is an urgency to get somewhere before the sun sets. We are flying very fast now and dropping lower, heading for the point of land where the sun touches the earth before it sets. We are flying lower and lower to the ground now. Wren is exhausted. We crash to the ground, I am face down in the dust. I am too tired to move. What I see from my position is the dust under my head. I tell Wren that I am reluctant to lift my head to look around. I tell her that I need some guidance to learn about relationships, especially my relationship with children. She seems exasperated with me. She has taken me so far and now I won't look around. I'm afraid she will fly away. She seems impatient. I still am unable to look around. I need to pick myself up and open my eyes. But I cannot move. I wait a long time. I feel that I won't listen to Wren or take her advice. She is too little. I feel like a rag without strength or will. I lie on the bare ground.

'Suddenly there is water seeping from somewhere. I still cannot move, I am face down and the water is rising. I feel I will drown. It is over me now. Surprisingly, I can still breathe. A child's boat just floated above me. Everything is growing up over me: lily pads, vines. There are more small boats. It is a fountain and it's in a city. I'm the monster that lives in the bottom of the fountain. I just lie here quietly and sometimes I just rise up and frighten little children. There are stories about me but no one really believes that it's true, that there is a monster that lives in the fountain at the city park. The children tell about the monster, that it is fierce and that it rises up out of the water. But no one really believes them.

'Suddenly I find myself alone with a small child, a boy. He is floating a sailboat on the water above me. I rise out of the water. I am ugly and frightening. He screams when he sees me and runs crying to his babysitter. She scolds him and slaps his face. She jerks him by the hand and takes him away.

'I am also . . . the fountain is big. The pool is flat and calm and dark. I am also the stone statue that is in the centre of the fountain. The statue is like a goddess. She is carved out of a grey stone and she is very beautiful. She has stars around her head and her body is draped with cloth that flows around her although it too is carved from stone. Her right hand is extended outward and that is what the water flows from that fills the pool. Her hand is small and beautifully carved. And I am the goddess as well. When I am the statue I can't move. I can't move. I am what brings the people. I am what brings the children. I . . . it feels like I . . . the statue is paralysed. As soon as I am the statue I am paralysed. I cannot move. I can make no changes. The pain of not moving lasts a long, long time.

'I feel like the only thing that would help me move is if the monster would come up to the bottom of the statue and somehow get inside. The statue is very tall and made of stone. I don't know what my fear is. The monster scares the children. I am afraid if the monster goes up into the statue she will hurt the children. I don't know this to be true but she might hurt the children. The desire to move overcomes the fear. It is happening. The moster is inside and she can move. Her right hand comes down to her side. She moves her legs, walks over and steps over the edge, out of the water. And she doesn't know if she is going to be destructive.

'Wren is waiting up in a tree. She flies down now and perches on the statue's right arm. The statue strokes her feathers. It seems like a good sign. I am the statue but I am also able to stand a little distance away and watch what is happening. The statue is walking down a path and the little bird is perched on her shoulder, her right shoulder. It feels good to walk after being stationary for so long. There are roses in the park and little children. She walks by and lifts her hand to acknowledge them. She is trying it out, how it feels to move around. People notice her because she still looks like a statue but she is walking. They want to touch her skin because it looks like it would be very cold like stone. The statue and the monster don't make a bad combination. She can walk around, move, but people aren't afraid of her. The monster feels a little safer.

'I ask Wren how I can learn from this feeling. She doesn't answer but instead shows me that there is a hole in the bottom of the statue's foot. She is allowing the monster to drain out of the hole. And I can't move. The monster is allowed back in and I can move. The little bird is saying that the monster needs somehow to permeate the stone so it can't drain out. I don't know how to do this.'

'Allow it to happen.'

'It is very hard to allow, very painful. I ask Wren, "Why is it so hard? What do I lose?" There is no answer but I feel the fusion happening.

'I am sitting on a park bench. I look like the statue. I have the same cloth draped around me but everything is real: my skin, the cloth, the stars around my head. Wren is sitting on my shoulder. I am sitting with my arms stretched along the back of the bench. An old man with a dark overcoat sits next to me. He's got a misshapen kind of hat that looks like it's been worn for about forty years. His hair is straight and grey. He's feeding some birds and I watch. Wren hops off my shoulder and goes over and sits on his knee to get some seeds. There are children and birds at his knees. The old man talks to me. He says, "I am your guide to teach you about feeding birds and children." He says his name is Thorne.

'I feel like I need to sit on the bench with him awhile and feel human and ask him a few questions. I ask him if he ever hurts children. He says, "You can never hurt children if you are fully alive and fully human." He's sort of grizzly. He has a sort of alertness. I ask Thorne how he stays fully human. He says he has always been human. He says some people are and some people aren't. He said if he'd been a statue he would probably just practise being human as much of the time as he could until he got used to it. He says, "It is a good way, to stay alert and to be outdoors with people and with children. And be human through your hands. Touch things." I hug him when he says that and he looks right at me for the first time. Before he has looked only at the birds. He has a long nose. His eyes are deep set in his head and they are a very light blue. I am startled by his looking. I ask again how I can practise being human. He continues to look at me and says, "You don't have to practise being human. You just *are* human. All you have to do is feel it." He stands up to leave and he takes my hand. He bows elaborately like he grew up in a time when people were formal. He bows very low as he takes my hand. And then he kisses me on the cheek and says I should come and visit him again. Wren stays on his shoulder. Wren is leaving too. I say goodbye to them both. And I feel sort of new. I want to sit here on a park bench and feel the new humanness while I watch them walk away down the path.'

14.

ISOL AND THE SUNFLOWER

'I'm in a place that has several images and there's confusion as to what to look at and so I think I'll just describe the whole thing. It's a bank of a stream and it's a narrow, a very narrow stream. It seems to be in the bottom of a canyon. It has high walls and the banks of the stream also seem to be quite steep. I'm standing in the canyon right on the bank of the stream and I look down into the stream and it's just a trickle of water.

'Another part of the landscape is a big sunflower. It must be August and the sunflower is just past its full flowering. It's still got petals on it but a couple of petals have fallen off, and the seeds have started to erupt from the surface like they do. And that sunflower is very tall. It's taller than I am. It's right next to me on the bank. It seems to be the only vegetation.'

'Ask the sunflower if it is your guide.'

'I ask it and it does some things. It doesn't talk back to me but one petals falls and some seeds erupt from the centre and fall on the ground. So it feels like it communicated to me but . . .'

'Ask it if it can speak.'

'It says, "I can signal".'

'Ask it if it is your guide.'

'It nods.'

'Ask it if it can show you what you need to know about fulfilling your potential.'

'It nods again.

'It indicates that we should go down the bank and I don't know if there's a canoe or something to get on the river. It seems to be mobile. It doesn't have to stay in the earth.'

'Let it lead you where it needs to take you.'

'It seems to have taken on some human qualities. It has little roots that look like feet, and the leaves . . . I can take one of the leaves and it has the feel of a hand. And we're going down this bank to this tiny stream. There's a big lily pad on the stream and it's like a boat, big enough to hold us, so that's what we're doing. It's very narrow but it's wide enough.

'We're now floating down deeper into the canyon. It feels murky like it's hard to see.'

'Ask the sunflower where it's taking you.'

'It says to a wider part of the river.

'I have a sense of not quite trusting it.'

'Express that to it.'

'It just sort of shrugs. I think it's not the sunflower I don't trust. I don't trust the journey.'

'Express that to it.'

'It says, "Just watch. Just pay attention." '

'There are little streams coming out of the rocks in the canyon. They're coming down to this central stream and it starts getting bigger and bigger. It's kind of frightening because the lily pad is thick and it was all right for a little tiny stream but it's a little precarious. I'm going fast, and downhill. Rocks. A whirlpool.

'There are all those whirlpools now. It feels like we're just going in between them but they have the ability to suck us down in it. It's a . . . It's a vast area of whirlpools and we seem to be going between them, but . . .'

'Ask the sunflower what they are.'

'I don't understand what he says. He says, "Little deaths. All little deaths."

'It feels like I'm up on a cliff and I'm looking down. I can see myself and the sunflower on the lily pad going through the water and all the whirlpools.'

'Allow yourself to be both places.'

'The horse, Isol, [1] seems to be up on a cliff, too, looking down like I just . . . I casually have my arm around the horse's neck and I'm just watching, and the part of me that's down on the river doesn't see clearly at all. It seems like it's confusing, it's . . . there's no direction and it's dark and . . . it's just luck. It feels like luck that the whirlpools are avoided.

'The part of me that's up on the canyon is emotionless, just watching, and up ahead there is a narrow place in the river, and the lily pad with the sunflower and me wants to go through that narrow place. It's a little better, the river's a little straighter, but I'm not sure, standing up above, if I like it. There seems to be something about direction. It feels like standing up there with Isol I'm looking down and thinking, "Well, they'll probably make it if they go in the right direction."'

'Is there anything you need to ask Isol?'

'It comes to my mind to ask him what he's doing there.

'He just said, "I came to watch how things are going." He seems to be very strong but very passive. And that's how I feel up on the rock, too, very receptive.

'I am up on the cliff but when I find myself going back down to be with the part of myself that's on the lily pad, it makes my . . . I feel anxious, I feel like my heart's beating fast, I feel . . . I don't know if it's fear. I'm going to go down there and see if I can figure it out. I can't think, that's the problem. The lily pad goes around and around. It's like it's on the edge of a whirlpool and it goes around and around, and it's almost like I feel dizzy and I can't think.'

'Ask the sunflower about it.'

'He says to take him by the stem and plunge him down into the water and the spinning will stop. So I do, and it's sort of like I use him for an oar, or a rudder. It takes an incredible amount of strength to hold him there. The flower is still out of the water, I guess I'll talk to him.

'I stop spinning so crazily.

'He says, "Now you have the will and the power to go through that narrow place in the river." And that's what I feel, like I could go through that and not stay in this confusing place, so I'm guiding myself. The rocks are very steep on either side of the river and it's narrow but it seems like it's very different. I can see through it. It's very different on the other side. It's sunnier and the water's clearer, and so that's what I'm doing, heading in that direction. It seems to be very slow, too slow.

'I'm going to go back up on the cliff to see if I can see what the problem is.

'I can see from the cliff there's a problem, but I can't see what it is.'

'Ask Isol.'

'I ask him. It feels incredibly emotional to ask. And Isol becomes . . . he isn't standing still any more, he becomes . . . just alive, he's pawing the ground and he's rearing up. He doesn't answer my question.'

'Ask him what you need to do.'

'Oh, he seems to . . . it's not clear. Let me see what he says. I'm up there with him and he's rearing and pawing the ground. I'm just standing a little ways away, watching him and watching myself down below just not quite going through the canyon.'

'What do you need to do?'

'He says that when I'm divided I'm not strong enough. I need to go down there.

'I don't just miraculously go down there like I came up, I have to crawl down there on the rocks.

'It feels like now when I'm on the lily pad I feel much stronger. I feel like I have the advantage of having been up on the canyon wall so I can see what I need to do. And it feels like all I have to do is to row with the sunflower, and it takes quite a bit of strength, but all I need to do is just see the direction, and just do it. It's very easy to row in whatever direction I choose, so that's what I'll do, just go through the narrow place in the canyon. The sunflower is very strong and makes a very good oar.

'It's interesting that the river seems to go uphill. Isol's up on the cliff and I wave to him and he's encouraging. It's like that's what the stamping's about, he's just encouraging.

'Now I'm in the narrow part of the river and I feel like there's some kind of misconception. I thought the water would be smooth there and it's not smooth. It feels like there's a waterfall or something. I feel like . . . like I don't know what to do, and . . . let me see.'

'Ask the sunflower.'

'Well, the sunflower said just discard the lily pad and . . . the sunflower is taking the shape of a log, it feels like he thinks if I just hang on to him we'll go down the waterfall. I feel confused about it. I don't know what the waterfall means. I feel like it's an impasse.'

'What are you going to do?'

'Well, it feels like I've a couple of choices . . . trying to go back through the whirlpools, which doesn't really seem like a good choice, or hang on to the sunflower and see if I can survive the waterfall. It seems like those are the two choices.'

'Which are you going to take?'

'It just feels obvious that I'll take the waterfall.'

'Good.'

'In fact, I feel cocky about it. I feel like I'm just going to sit on the log . . . I mean I'm not even clinging to it. I have my legs wrapped around it and I just . . . ride the waterfall, kind of shrieking.' [laughs]

'Good. Go with it.'

'Well, it feels like quite a ride. It feels very fast and very directional, although I don't know where it's going. But it's not like the whirlpools. It feels very exciting. It feels very risky.

'I wish I knew where I was going. I say that and the sunflower says, "You need to pay attention to where we are." And that seems to be true. It feels like it takes a lot of awareness to stay upright.

'I have a feeling of heaviness in my chest. I'm gonna ask about it.

'The sunflower says it's because I'm not fully experiencing the ride. I don't quite understand that.

'It feels like suddenly I am overcome with fear and I change my position. I'm clinging to the sunflower and I have my eyes closed. I'm not looking at anything that's happening.'

'Tell that to the sunflower and ask its advice.'

'He says if I won't look at what's happening I can feel what's happening.'

'Feel it then, fully. Go directly into it.'

[long pause]

'What's happening?'

'I have a feeling like it's just hurdling . . . like I'm just really . . . losing my feeling.'

'Stay with everything. Don't lose anything. Stay with it, use your will to stay with it.'

'It feels like I'm . . . like I don't wanna hurt. I'm . . . it feels like . . . like I'm doing everything to keep from hurting. It feels like it's just so hard. I think I'll go up on the cliff and see if I can see things clearly. It feels like I'm in the water and I'm being crushed around on huge rocks, I'm out of control . . .'

'Tell the sunflower what's happening.'

'He says I can go up on the rocks to see, but I need to stay down here, too. So that's what I'll do.'

'What happens down below that you don't have up on the rocks?'

'What happens down below is that I can't see clearly.'

'But you can feel.'

'Uh huh.' [crying]

'Up above you can see but not feel, and below you can feel but not see clearly.'

'And I thought . . . I thought I could just come down and see clearly and it worked for a tiny time.'

'And to split the two is to split your energy.'

'Uh huh. Uh huh.'

'Where do you need to be right now?'

'Ohhh, I just am neither place. Let me see who I can ask. It feels like I can ask Isol.'

'Go above. Ask him, and see what's happening.'

'He says that they don't have to be so far apart. It feels like he has the ability to fly down and fly just above the water.'

'Can you ride on his back while he does that?'

'That's what I'm doing. We're able to fly just above the water. I . . . I'm both places, and I'm hanging on to the sunflower and hurdling down this stream and I'm underwater and I . . . the part of me that's riding on Isol can see myself clearly underwater but I feel detached from it. I don't even understand it.'

'What about the part that's underwater? Is that part aware of Isol up above?'

'Uh huh.'

'Okay, good. Go back to the part underwater.'

'I'm worried about not being able to breathe.'

'Talk to the sunflower about it.'

'The sunflower indicates I could stop spinning around under-

water if I just do a few things, like crawl up a little closer to the
flower and stabilize the stem with my feet. And it seems like
. . . I said he but it seems suddenly apparent that the flower's a
she. It feels like it's just a little control, just a slight different
manoeuvre and I wouldn't be spinning so violently not being able
to breathe. So I do that. I'm still hanging on to the sunflower stem
but my face is right next to the flower and I'm floating on my
back. And I can see Isol right above me. It feels like I'd like to
reach out and grab his foot or something.'
    'Tell that to the sunflower.'
    'She said I need to stay in the water and just see Isol, and so
I do that. And it feels like what happens is that just . . . just seeing
I stay in contact with the water but I'm not underneath it. Before
my face was the only thing out of it, but now all my body's just
floating on top and I feel like it's Isol that keeps me out of the
water. There's some kind of magnetic pull that I feel.
    'It's funny. I feel connected with Isol but I don't feel connected
with the part of me that's riding him.'
    'Do you feel connected with the sunflower?'
    'Yeah, it's like we're floating together, and Isol's acting like a
magnet so we're floating *on* the water. I'm aware that part of me
is riding on Isol, but I can't see that part.'
    'Go up and be that part.'
    'All right. It feels like what I am doing is looking way out on
to the horizon and I feel very alert.'
    'Can you see the part of you that's in the water?'
    'I look down and I feel, I don't know if it's disgust or what it is.'
    'Tell that to Isol.'
    'I'm gonna tell him again. He said something and I didn't hear
what he said. I'm saying to him, "We could fly anywhere on the
horizon but you're wasting your energy pulling this part of me
and this flower along." And I'm gonna see what he says.'
    [sighs]
    'What's happening?'
    'Isol is chastising me. He's saying that is the best part, that is
the valuable part. [crying] And I'm going to ask him why it's such
a drag. Why can't . . . why can't the flower come up and ride?
    'He says, "Why can't you go down and trust?"'
    'I'm gonna see what that would feel like. [crying] I'm not sure

how it happened but it feels like both of me merged. It's sort of like a picture out of focus, and there are really two images but they're like . . . if . . . if you're looking you could hardly tell it's not quite right but it's almost right.'

'See what you can do to focus them, like a sterescope.'

'What's happened is I . . . I'm out of the water and I'm floating in the air, and I'm right behind Isol. I've got the flower in my hand, it's like a big . . . like a big walking stick or . . . or staff. I'm in motion, and it feels like if I just use the staff I can leap on to the back of the horse. That's what I'm going to do.

'Oh, it just works, it works very well. I'm riding very fast, and I'm holding the staff, and it's a wonderful feeling.'

'Are the two fully merged?'

'Uh huh. I feel like . . . I feel like a warrior. I'm riding up on the hills and I'm able to stay on the horse easily.

'There's something about the movement that feels important. It feels like as soon as I would stop then the parts of me would just split in half again, but as long as I'm moving they'll stay together. I ask Isol about it and he says that it's enough to learn what it feels like, and that I should remember what it feels like.

'I'm galloping just really fast. There's a high ridge. I am just . . . screaming, out of some kind of strength. Then I stop on the ridge and I don't fall apart.

'I feel like I'm done for today. I feel like I'll climb off Isol, and leave the staff there, too.'

'Thank them both for being your guides today. Ask them when you should see them again.'

'As I walk away I have a sense of them belonging together. I left the staff next to Isol. He said I could come back any time.'

Note:
1.   Isol is a winged white horse who appeared as a guide in a visualization undertaken four months previously. He had not appeared since then, and appears now spontaneously.

PART FIVE

AN ESOTERIC JOURNEY

The meaning of an inner journey is deeper than the individual himself. Or — the part we call 'I' has deep roots whose existence we have forgotten. We are like a plant who thinks of itself as only those parts which are visible above ground. It is no wonder that we feel unanchored, have lost our relationship to the earth, and can no longer easily drink from that well of deeper nurturing.

In this section an individual who already possesses considerable depth, sees how deep he goes, with some surprises.

15.

JOURNEY THROUGH
THE CHAKRAS

I met Robert Standard one afternoon at the college where I was teaching. He was a physician associated with a holistic health centre in a neighbouring city, and was doing some consulting with our Department of Nursing.

My first impression of Robert was that he was quiet and serious, and although probably near my age, he looked at the same time both younger and older. He had a tall, very lean frame, that he carried in a stooped way, as if he had spent many hours poring over books, or had gotten into the habit of conversing with people at their level. His stooped posture and angular body along with greying hair gave him an old appearance, but his open, rather puzzled facial expression contrasted markedly and gave him a look of being barely past adolescence.

I first met him at a formal meeting in the afternoon and was surprised to see him again that evening in a local delicatessen where I often stopped after a busy day. During a casual conversation over sandwiches, I learned of his interest in visualization and imagery. He asked about the possibility of exploring his own chakra system[1] with the use of visualization. I had at that time very little knowledge of chakras other than that they were energy centres in the body posited by some eastern theoretical views, but I said I would be willing to assist him with his exploration. We agreed to meet the next day in my office.

I took Robert initially through a standard relxation procedure. What follows is a transcript of his communication to me during that session.

'. . . Go to the place where you can meet a guide who will take you through your chakra system and also show you where energy needs to flow more freely.'

'I am butter that is just melting. And the butter drips down through a little hole. I'm going down into that hole. It looks almost like a navel, there's something almost umbilical about it.

'There's some bushes along one side and I climb down those bushes. It's like a cave that goes straight down but these bushes are very sturdy, like they've been used for climbing before, and they form a ladder going down and so I climb down. And then the opening which was very small, not much bigger than me, begins to widen out into what feels like a larger chamber, and I continue climbing down.

'Down inside I'm standing next to a lake that feels like it's made out of glass, it's that still and that smooth. In fact, it looks like one of those scenes of a diorama where a glass or a mirror is used as a pool of water.

'Ha. Ha. I call out and say, "Is my guide there?", and a voice answers, "No, you have to explore around a bit first."

'So I walk around the pool, and then it occurs to me to look into it.

'I look into it and the reflection I see looks kind of like the Wolf Man, the face is all hair. And I ask if he's my guide, and he kind of laughs a fiendish laugh and says no, he's not. And I ask him who he is and he says, "I am a reflection of the part of you that you fear."

'I ask him, "How can I get to know you better?"

'And he says, "You've been exploring me little by little."

'And I tell him, "I really do want to get to know you."

'And he says, "I know."

'And I reach out to touch him and hold him and he just kind of melts. He's very sad and afraid, timid inside. And all of this looking like a wolf is . . . a protectiveness. He shrinks inside into something that looks like it's either a doll or a puppy. And he's just a really friendly little puppy. So I hold him and rock him back and forth.

'Then I get an image of my mother holding me when I was an infant and rocking me in front of our fireplace. And I really loved it. Then I see my father telling me that I'm too big for her to hold me and rock me and I'm very sad, and I'm not big, I'm just a little kid, you know, maybe two or three years old. But he forbids her to rock me any more.

'And I really hurt. It's like I've lost the place where I was most fully nurtured. And it's very much of a conflict, because on the one hand I do want to be big and mature and looked up to, and on the other hand I still want to be that little baby that's rocked and comforted. I'm very sad and perplexed about that.

'Now I see myself at the age that I am, fully grown, and her holding me and rocking me. It seems very silly. Ooooooh. And then I see that in my heart she's there and she's still rocking me as an infant. And that's good. That's where it needs to happen.

'It feels like I've regained that warmth and security that was there so much when she'd hold me and rock me. [deep sigh] And it feels like that's where I first hurt, that's where my heart was first injured, at my being forbidden to sit in her lap any more.

'Now I see that she's rocking in rhythm to the beat of my heart. And I feel like the infant who feels warm and cosy and wrapped in . . . a sheepskin. Totally protected.

'And somebody says, "Now you can go to your guide."

'Hmmmm. I'm still carrying with me that rocking chair, in my heart, with her rocking me as an infant in it. Ooooooh. I suddenly realize that I've been looking for that on the outside and I have to really seek it on the inside.

'Hmmmm. Now I see that there's a tunnel that leads away from that large chamber, off to one side, kind of at an angle. And I go down this tunnel, which . . . it's illuminated but I don't know where from. It's like that was a very old sadness that needed to be healed.

[long pause]

'There's some brighter light up ahead.

[pause]

'I get to a chamber and there's an old man. He has a white robe on. He's very old . . . but totally alive. He has long white hair and a white beard, and yet his eyebrows are very dark, very black, and he has very deep, dark eyes. And I ask him if he's my guide, and he says, yes, he is. I ask him what I can call him, and he says, "You may call me Jacob."

'I ask him if he will take me on a journey where I can learn more about my chakras and if he will help me clear the pathways so that my energy can flow more freely, and he says, yes, he will.

'He tells me that there had to be some healing in my heart before he could do that, and that was the reason for the other chamber.

'He takes me over and he shows me a small model of a city, or at least of some buildings, and he's going to make me very small so I can go through some of the rooms in the buildings. And he becomes very small with me.

'We start out standing in a very open courtyard. It's kind of centred. Hah! Then we go down a manhole in the street, which surprises me. And he tells me that many people think that the sewers are dark and ugly, but that they are not. They're very essential and very beautiful.

'So we walk along and there is water flowing along in this sewer, but it's very clean, very pure water. The tunnel is arched and it seems to be made of glazed tile, beautiful glazed tile.

'We get to a place where there is a door, barred. It's a door made out of bars like you'd find in a prison. And he slides it open and says, "This is a major impediment." And so he slides it open, pushes it open. He locks it open, and says, "There. Now things can move more freely here."

'And we go in and it's like we're inside a cupola, like the Taj Mahal. Very bright. Very beautiful. Very pure in there. And it's round with some windows high up. All I can see is sky as I look through them. And a beautiful domed ceiling.

'And there's something right in the centre. There is . . . oh, uh huh. It's a fountain, right in the centre. And it wasn't running when we went in and then it starts, with water kind of flooding out of it and then spraying up, like a fountain, and falling in around . . . it also looks like an eye, a round eye. Then the water falls into this surrounding . . . it's a surrounding . . . I don't know what to call it . . . a surrounding bath which then flows out in the direction that we came from.

'He says, "This is your first chakra."

'He says, "All of your chakras are holy places."

'And I ask him, "What do I have to do here to keep the water flowing?"

'He says, "Trust yourself."

'The fountain can flow up into various configurations, get higher or lower, and form various designs as it flows out. And he says the design is unimportant, the important thing is the flow.

'The place is clean as can be, just beautifully polished. I see now that there is a bench around the wall, a bench in a circle. And it's like this, taken together with the tunnel through which we came, looks something like a keyhole. And he says to me, "We are the keys which are unlocking this."

'Oh, and I can see that the fountain can get so big that it just fills the whole chamber. Uh huh . . . and as it does the whole chamber becomes tremendously luminous, just glowing. It's not that it's full of water, but that it's full of spray from the fountain. And I feel the water, but the water seems to be more like mercury, but also very warming.

'And he and I, also, as we stand there, begin to glow as if we were both just ruddy, healthy, really vitally alive. Just glowingly alive. Standing in there with him I feel remarkably energized.

'And he says, "Good. Let's move on now."

'And we go out the way we came. The fountain continues to flow. It seems to pulsate. It gets great big and fills the chamber, and then it gets very small. But all the time it continues to flow.

'And as we leave we get in a boat. It's a beautiful wooden boat, beautifully made, beautifully crafted, pure wood, unpainted. It's varnished but unpainted. And we float. We have a couple of oars but we more or less just float along in this boat. The water's much higher and much swifter now.

'And as were floating along in this tunnel we reach another locked iron gate. Bars, made out of bars. And again, he takes a key and unlocks it, and opens it by sliding it off into the wall, and locks it open. And he says, "That was another impediment."

'And that, then, lets us into a very square room, just like a perfect cube. Big. Very big but square, perfectly square. All dimensions are the same, height, width, and depth.

'And close to the corner . . . each corner . . . looks like a round

thing . . . looks like a barstool . . . and these . . . then . . . grow,
very fast, like mushrooms . . . and blossom into flowers, great
big flowers. Four different colours. There's a red, a yellow, a blue
and a green.

'And he says to me, "And this is your second chakra."

'And he tells me that the added water that has flowed in here
had helped those flowers to grow and blossom. And he lets me
smell each one, and each one has a different fragrance.

'Right in the middle of that chamber there is a round opening
into which the water pours. Uh huh . . . oh . . . I see now, yes.
The water, as it enters this cube, flows around to all of the corners.
But then it also flows . . . ooooh, yes . . . it flows down into that
centre hole, also. And then it suddenly fills up with water, very
high, except for the blossoms, which look like they're floating,
although they are still on their stems. And then from there the
water all rushes to that centre, flows there, like a whirlpool. Like
there's a flow going through here, very fast, now. So he and I,
in our boat, go around and around in the whirlpool. It goes in
a clockwise direction. And we go deeper and deeper.

'But then it's . . . it feels like we suddenly pop out very high
up. We've been going down, from the standpoint of the cubicle
chamber, but then when we come out it's like we have popped
up into a light bulb or a balloon or something spherical that shines
into the sky. And it is just luminous.

'And we are there inside of this . . . it could be . . . I don't know
what it is. I've been seeing it from the outside and so now I go
inside of it . . . now I see that I'm inside with him, and from here
there is a very powerful force, like radiation which just radiates
from this globe in all directions.

'And he tells me, "One of the things you need to learn is to
aim this radiation, to aim this power."

'And I ask him, "How can I do that?"

'And he shows me that on the inside there's a little lever that
can go all the way around. By moving that lever I can concentrate the beam. It doesn't stop the radiation that goes off
in all directions, but there develops a particular concentration
of radiation going in one direction. So I can aim it by moving
the lever all the way around. And then by pulling it down or up
I can also aim it this way, so that I have 360 degree directionality.

'And he says, "Whatever you aim it at will be affected." And he tells me that I have to be very tempered in what I deliberately aim it at. It's not a thing to play with, but a fairly serious thing.

'Hm. Also, there's a grate on the bottom and he removes it. And light just flows in and floods the whole inside when the grate is removed. And he puts it over to one side and locks it over to that side. In fact, there seems to be a niche that is just made for storing the grate.

'And he tells me, "Of course, this is just the initial tour, and really getting all of these things working may take a little more time."

'I seem kind of puzzled and ask, "Okay, where do we go from here, how do we get out of here?" There seems to be no passageway, no path other than the one through which we came, which was the strangely inverted thing, of going down and then finding ourselves kind of up . . . up in a tower.

'And he tells me, "Don't be in such a hurry."

'And I tell him, "But Teresa's time is limited."

'Then Jacob laughs and says, "Ask her." '

I tell Robert that I have plenty of time.

'Okay. I tell Jacob you said there's plenty of time and he says, "I knew it." He's a beautiful old man.

[pause]

'Oh . . . he wants me to practise on this a little . . . directing the beam . . . and I see that whatever I aim it at either melts . . . or is drawn closer. And there are certain things that I'm scared of aiming it at. Or certain directions I'm afraid of aiming it . . . kind of a feeling like if I aim it in those directions I'll just be devoured.

'And he says, "Yes, you have to be willing to be changed." Not so much a willingness to change as a willingness to be changed.

'So I try it all around and then I aim it straight up . . . and it is remarkably powerful, like that is the highest concentration it can have. Straight up to the sky. Straight up to Heaven.

'And we travel out on the beam, and the end of it is flared out like a trumpet. And it's also kind of like were floating on it. And it carries us to a totally different level.

'And we just kind of lounge around up there on it, as if we were on the beach, or something. And he's pointing out to me how

there's always been an undercurrent . . . of edginess. From up there I see it, I feel it, very clearly. It's like there's a very thin layer of edginess . . . which somehow is very . . . very fundamental to my identity . . . and yet I've been totally blind to it. This is the first time I've really seen it . . . and it's like a nervousness . . . like an intensity . . . like an anxiety . . . it's like an extremely compacted emotion. I feel it particularly in my arms, in my hands, in my wrists . . . And as I see that, as I feel it, as I experience it . . . it's as if the thing, which feels like it's about the thickness of a sheet of paper, becomes transparent. And then suddenly it begins to melt or dissolve . . . it diffuses down into what feels like humus . . . beautiful deep dark soil . . . pure and clean . . . rich. Ooooh. And he shows me that when this was there as the . . . sheet of paper . . . that it was equivalent to a block . . . a blockage . . . something very driven about it . . . very driving. But as I let it suffuse down into the rich earth it becomes very generative, like it is energy from which all kinds of things can grow. As it sinks down it gets finer and finer, smaller and smaller, little droplets, like a very fine mist. And it nurtures the soil and makes it fertile. That soil had been sterile before this . . . still rich and beautiful, but sterile. And he relates that layer, not the soil but the layer of edginess, to a . . . an angst . . . a . . . dread.
    [pause]
    'And it feels like that earth, now, is just seething with potential. It can grow anything . . . now. And out of the very centre of it a great big flower begins to grow. It's just like a very delicately shaded pink carnation, with its leaves and stalk. It's very beautiful. And now other flowers pop out on it, very beautiful, fully blossomed. It turns into a stalk just heavy with flowers. It just continues to grow up and up and up, infinitely.
    'And I ask him, "What's that?"
    'And he says, "That is the beauty of your power." And he points out to me how delicate it is . . . and at the same time how totally infinite.
    'As we're standing there around that flower he says to me suddenly — it surprises me — he says to me suddenly, "We are now in the fourth chakra."
    'And I'm confused because I expect . . . I guess because of the turns that the flow has taken, and I expect them to be all nice and orderly and logical.

'He says, "Don't worry about that."

'And then he takes me up that stalk, with all its flowers. And at the very top there is a bright red rose. Here are all of these delicate pink carnations, it's just loaded with them all the way up the stalk, and then right in the centre of them, right at the very top of the stalk, is just a deep, deep red rose.

'And we jump into the middle of it, and it feels like there are some waves going out from that. In fact, he seems to go in one direction out on one of the waves and I go out in another direction. I don't quite know what to do so I just float along on it. It's very strange, it seems to be invisible and yet it has a very definite substance to it. It seems intangible and yet it very definitely exists. Hah.

'Oh. And I see him now. All of these waves that go out form something like a funnel, a dish, and, uh, radiate out. And he comes around now to where I am and then the two of us continue around from there and we go higher and higher.

'It feels like we're just floating in the sky and yet, there is this very definite something that's supporting us. Uh huh.

'I'm very concerned that we're not going in a straight direction. And he's amused with my attempts to make everything logical and . . . and conform to my ideas.[2] It's very obvious that I don't know where to go or what to do. And he's totally relaxed and humoured by my . . . by my concerns.

'And suddenly I become aware of how concerned I am. In becoming aware of that concern I suddenly experience it as . . . as . . . funny. Like I've been so wrapped up in that concern that I haven't been able to see beyond it.

'And as we float around, seemingly suspended in air and yet very definitely supported, he whispers, "Be quiet, somebody might hear us. Now we are in the fifth chakra."

'And I'm totally stupefied because . . . well, I expected it to be more of a definite something and it seems to be . . . a very definite intangible . . . but also very free, and beautiful freedom, and beautiful clarity. And he's tickled by my consternation.

'And it feels like there's a very fine rain, a very fine mist that's falling from above. But it's not water . . . there's something both silvery and gold about it. And we follow it upward, just . . . moving upward, effortlessly. Levitating. It feels like we have left

. . . left that thing that was supporting us, and we travel upward without any support, without any need of support. Just travelling up through this very fine mist that's falling.

[long pause]

'And he tells me, "You're going to have some trouble now because all the way along we've been packaging this in terms of something that you know from experience, and we're going to move up to a place where you can't compare this to previous experience."

'I keep seeing some clouds at the top from which this fine mist flows and yet we never seem to reach them. And then suddenly we break through them.

'And it's very bright. And there are some strange, intangible beings which feel like some very strange creatures, and yet, themselves are . . . have no substance to them, they're purely ethereal, purely spiritual, and yet very strange creatures, like mixtures of animals that I might have some familiarity with. I have trouble getting ahold of them because I've been trying to compare them to animals that I know, and so it's like I can only see a part of them at any one time, the part that compares to some other animal, and yet I know that I have to see this thing as a whole, as a totality.

'And it's like we are ringed with these beings. And the beings are all interconnected and yet each one is independent, is an individual.

'And it feels like this ring together is itself a creature, is itself a unitary entity.

'And he says to me, "Now we are in the sixth chakra."

'Huh . . . and he indicates to me that my tendency to try to put these beings, to try to categorize them as something that I have already previously experienced, that thing that I'm doing right there, he says, "This is what you call the intellect, this continuous attempt to transform these very intangible beings into something known."

'And it's very interesting. It's like that . . . the intangible beings themselves are the intuitive element and the attempt to see them definitely as something already known is the intellectual element. And they . . . the intellectual element exists almost in frustration relative to this other . . . and has evolved from it, or evolved relative to it, so that the intangible creatures that constitute this doughnut shaped being are just a much more basic source of the intellect. And he indicates to me that the intellect is doomed to frustration because it's trying to do something that it can never complete.

'Ooooooh. And he shows me now that those places where I had that edginess and also the great concern are directly related to this frustration on the part of the intellect, are kind of born out of it. And he also shows me that this is what Camus was getting at in *The Myth of Sisyphus*, the man rolling the boulder up the hill which would then roll back down again.

'And then he gets me to see that there's no need to be frustrated by the intellect, that I can understand it as similar to petals on a flower which grow and then are shed almost as quickly as they grow, are very subtle, are very . . . are very momentary, disappear as soon as they pop forth.

'He shows me how very closely related this is to language. Mmmmm. Further frustration arises from trying to turn the spoken word into the written word. When the word is only spoken you can see it growing and then falling away. As soon as it's spoken, it disappears. And when we write something down it's as if we are trying to capture that live petal, but all we have left is a dried specimen, its life is gone. Uhhh. He shows me that the way out of this is to be centred in the intuitive, and I see it now as a ring of petals on the outside of the intuitive.

'Then it's as if we just move straight up and are on the outside of the universe, and the universe being totally circulous, with everything contained within it.

'And as we sit there on the top of this globe which contains everything, he says, "*Now we are in the seventh chakra.*"

'And it's just totally awesome. [whispered]

[long pause]

'Ha ha. I look at him and I say, "I don't know what to say."

'And he says, "I know."

'And we just kind of sit there, in touch with each other, holding hands. And we just glow while we are sitting there. And I say to him, "It's awesome."

'And he says, "I know."

'And the universe itself is whole . . . completely circular thing, itself is just glowing, and is . . . uh . . . just a beautiful, an inexpressibly magnificent, living entity. Just . . . it's existence is just totally mysterious . . . and yet totally remarkable.

'And I ask him, "What should I do now?"'

'And he says, "Just feel it."'

[long pause]

'And he says to me, "This is the Being of which you are a part."'

'Hmmm. And I tell him, "Everybody's a part of this Being."'

'He says, "Nothing exists that's not a part of this."'

'It is an organism that is just . . . just so precise, and so . . . so intricately put together, yet so totally alive, that it's just completely flabbergasting. It looks like a diatom.

[very long pause]

'I suddenly become aware in talking to him that I'm in a hurry, and that again, that's part of that edginess. [deep breath] And as soon as that hurriedness disappears then I become aware of . . . it's as if I kind of sink back down into the universe, as softly as if it were . . . just an immense marshmallow . . . and sink right back down here . . . OH, WOW!'

Notes:

1.   In later discussion with Robert he provided me with this summary of the chakra system.

> The first chakra is located at the base of the spine and is associated with the sex organs. Its function is grounding and survival. It is the source of energy which flows up the spine and through the remaining chakras.

> The second chakra is located in the abdomen and is associated with the intestines. It is the emotional centre.

> The third chakra is located at the level of the diaphragm and is the centre of power.

> The fourth chakra is the heart chakra and is associated with love and caring.

> The fifth chakra is the chakra of communication, located in the thyroid gland and speech centres.

> The sixth chakra is located in the head and has two parts, an intuitive level associated with the pineal gland, and an intellectual level associated with the frontal lobes.

The seventh chakra is the crown chakra, located above the head and associated with spiritual energy.

2.   Robert related to me later that his expectation of the visualization was that it would entail a journey through the physical body with visits to the different organs which have been classically associated with the chakras, and that he had been constantly surprised at the fact that the visualization did not follow his expectations.

16.

GUIDE TO POWER

Several weeks after the visualization I received a phone call from Robert Standard. He was calling from Seattle and had just visited a woman who was known for her 'aura readings'.[1] Although he had told her nothing of his recent visualization, the principal thing she had told him was that his third chakra, his power centre, was inverted. He had been quite amazed, recalling vividly the images he had experienced concerning his third chakra. She had performed something that she had called 'psychic surgery' on him with the purpose of correcting the inversion. In his description of the 'psychic surgery' he said that she had stood some distance from him and that there was no actual physical contact but that she had 'manipulated his energy' and that he had become aware of a definite body sensation in his midsection and had left feeling clear and relaxed. Robert was exuberant about this 'validation' of his visualization and we agreed to do another on his next trip to our city.

The visit came two weeks after his call. He arrived at our college, ostensibly to do some consulting, but he told me later, over dinner, that his primary purpose in scheduling the trip had been to do another visualization.

He seemed sombre and moody, and explained to me that he was dissatisfied with his position at the holistic health centre. He had joined the centre a little over a year ago, and although he supported it in theory, he felt that his own abilities were somehow not being fully utilized. He was feeling a vague need to change directions and was toying with the possibility of entering a residency programme in psychiatry. He was aware that his sense of dissatisfaction was long standing although it had never been previously articulated. He told me that he felt his earlier visualization and the psychic surgery had somehow allowed the dissatisfaction to surface.

After dinner we returned to my office at the college. Robert specifically requested that I help him get in touch with a 'guide to his power'. I led him through a relaxation sequence until he was in a place where he could meet his guide. This is Robert's description.

'I'm on the edge of my space and what I do initially is to ask to meet a guide to my power which is positive, generative, and which will help me do what I need to do from the very beginnings of my existence on this earth.

'The space is like a circle, and yet one edge of it is a little brighter than the rest, so that it's like a crescent moon. The crescent moon is kind of extended with a greyer circle. It's milk white. And the grey circle has some different shadings to it also, maybe a very faint shaded crescent on the edge of it also. My feeling is that I need to go right into the centre of all of that. And so I go.

'I sink right into the middle of it, or I get smaller and smaller so that it looks like I disappear right into the middle of it, and yet I know that I'm very tiny right there in the centre of it. So that I can see the moon and crescents as a circle and I'm a little tiny speck right in the centre of it.

'Now it feels like I am following that speck, that I am sinking into the centre, to see what the speck sees. And it's like there's a funnel, a gently turning funnel, not rotating, but the moon itself is gently rolling into a funnel, becoming a funnel itself, with a very gentle roll to it. And I'm going down the centre of that funnel. Going around, spiralling clockwise as I go deeper.

'I seem to be wearing a strange hat that feels something like a Robin Hood hat, but at the same time I'm wearing . . . I think it's called a ghi, it's a karate fighting robe.

'I keep going deeper and deeper into what seems like an endless funnel that'a almost like a hollowed out ear. Then I come out and land on some strange stuff that's kind of bouncy, red, and organic. Seems to be slightly quilted but I can't tell what the pattern is. And there's something like a trough that I sit in and continue to slide down, and it's deep red . . . feels like I'm inside of a body, feels like I've gone through a hypodermic needle inside of a body. And I'm also becoming aware that it feels like I'm in too much of a hurry. There's a certain intensity that makes things a little edgy. And as I become aware of that I seem to relax and slow down. I feel a tremendous amount of power on my left side, particularly in my left arm and hand.

'And now it feels like I'm just sitting waiting for something. I also feel myself changing as I sit and wait. It's like my power is being smoothed out, more constant throughout my being, less of an edge to it. It's a perplexing thing because I feel like I really am in a hurry, and yet, on the other hand, the only thing I can do is . . . is wait. And so as I wait I see that the feeling of hurriedness is itself a kind of power. And it feels like I need to become comfortable with that kind of power. So far I see nothing distinct around me, although there do seem to be some forms around, like a strange landscape that I've never seen before. It's made up of darker hues, blues, greens, all kinds of greyish shade but with an intensity all their own.

'Hmmmm. I suddenly become aware that I have been projecting some of that hurried feeling on to you, as if you were in a rush or in a hurry. Like I had to hurry to accommodate you. And I'm becoming aware of the origin of that in my past. Whenever my parents were ill at ease I would feel that coming from them. And now it's . . . I don't know . . . I see them there now, in a somewhat indistinct form, and I ask them, "Are you my guides?"

'And they say, "No." It's like they're ghosts.

'And I see something now that looks like it could be a beetle or it could be a jewel. And I think immediately of a scarab. And I ask that beetle, or that jewel, it looks like it might be a jewel set in a gold ring, but it's hazy and fuzzy . . . and yet there's a strange depth to it. I ask it, "Are you my guide?"

'And it says, "Well, yes and no."

'My feeling is that it is something that belongs to my guide.
And I ask it, "What am I to do with you?"

'And it says, "Tune in to me."

'And I see that it's a beetle with some finely etched colouration,
very distinct markings, beautiful deep grey and some rather bright
orange. And it's . . . I keep trying to compare it to beetles that
I've seen before, like ladybugs, but it's not that, and I have a feeling
that I've never seen this kind of beetle before. And I'm trying to
make it conform to what I've seen. It seems to be alive, but it
also seems to be a gem, stone, crystal. Then I become aware that
I've been seeing it as if it's in front of me in some depth, and it
occurs to me that I never seem to see things behind me.

'And as I realize that the ring chuckles, and it makes itself into
a loop and slips itself on a finger as if there were someone standing
behind me, someone very powerful, and someone who can reach
right through me. To him I am just insubstantial, in the sense of
being like air, or like a spirit rather than solid. So I feel this being
behind me, and I know even without asking, that he is my guide.

'And I ask him anyway, "Are you my guide?"

'And he is beautifully rich and full and . . . and deep and
spontaneous, and he laughs and says, "Oh, yes, yes, yes."

'He feels very much like Seth in the Seth books, that same kind
of depth and richness, and I ask him if he's Seth and he laughs
again and says, "No."

'I ask him if I will ever see him and he says, "Yes."

'I ask him when and he says, "Don't be in a hurry."

'And so I just stand there and feel him behind me, and he's bigger
than I am and kind of dark. And I can see one hand, his left hand
that has the ring on it. He's dark, not deeply dark, but tawny.
There's a kind of depth to the colour of his skin.

'And I see his right hand come around and it's like he's
embracing me. And he wraps his hands together and rubs them
together like somebody either making a wish or somebody being
satisfied with what they've done, or somebody having completed
something. And then he shakes them. It feels like he's been washing
his hands although there's no water there, and then he shakes
them dry.

'Now I'm becoming aware of his feet. They extend down very

far, so that my feet end at about the level of his knees. He's wearing shoes, nondescript shoes, featureless shoes, I should say. And black slacks.

'I realize that he's doing something with that thing that looks like handwashing and then shaking. He's doing something with energy, kind of the way my aura reader flings away energy with her hands. It's as if he's washing something in front of me. And I'm very aware that he's doing something with my power, right in front of me, like he's washing it clean, wringing it clean, purifying it in some way.

'And I'm very aware that his chin hovers right over my head. He's big, big. I ask him, "Should I do anything?"

'And he says, "Yes, watch."

'He says to me, "Not only am I a guide, but I will help you steer your power."

'And I ask him, "What are you doing now?", with reference to his handwashing.

'And he just says, "Humph."

'And I ask him if I'm ready to use my power, and he says, "Ohhh, yes."

'Now I see his hands, going like this, almost like he's raking through a beam with his fingers, starting close to me and then raking outwards. I . . . he's cleansing me, he's putting me together, energywise.

'And I start feeling something in my midsection and he chuckles at that. In fact, he's taking it and stretching it out, almost like milking a cow, or like pulling toffee, and making me very aware of it, and also, it's like he's pulling something out of my midsection. Pulling something out from inside of me. And I see it's not just one thing but it's . . . it's a number of thick . . . thick . . . thick things that are like dough, or like beams of light, or like fibres of some kind. Or like very thick pasta.

'And now it feels like he's putting something in my back right behind that, so that it comes all the way through me. And then I see that it's his . . . it's his power. He's putting it right in me and it comes right through me, comes right out in front. But it's not mine, it's really his.

'Now he's taking each of these beams and kind of stripping it and stretching it, like this. [Robert showed me with his hands]

'Now I become aware that some of these beams come from different parts of me. Here's one that comes from my heart, projects backward and loops around, enters my back, and comes out my midsection. I see that there's a whole row of these things, from my head all the way down, way down into my legs and feet, and also into my arms. And it's as if they all . . . project out backwards first, then loop around, are gathered together, and all then jut out in front of me. It feels very much like these have their origins in something akin to . . . to acupressure points.

'Aaaaahhhh. Then I see that it's places that are very sensitive, very perceptive, that pick up energy from the environment, from whatever's in front of me. I feel it at these places, the front, and then it's as if the energy itself that I pick up is carried through these loops and ultimately comes back out my front. So that I pick up the energy and then I'm capable of using it to do something in this whole power system that's coming out of my midsection. Like this forms a loop with the world, in terms of being aware of the world and then acting back on the world.

'Any single point in itself is not much, but it has the capacity to ignite all of these other points at the place where they join together, so that my response to whatever I can perceive can be remarkably powerful, remarkably amplified. And I see that these projections that go out from my midsection are infinitely long, and yet I can use them as if they were any length at all. To deal with something quite close, or farther away, or extremely distant. And that distance seems to be temporal as well as spacial.

'I've gotten so wrapped up in looking at this that I've forgotten about this being that's behind me, and I see now that he's standing back with his hand on his chin just watching me, chuckling at my . . . my being so wrapped up in this, in seeing this.

'It looks like that beam of fibres comes from him, but also comes from the world, and that I'm kind of a loop with the world then, that the world acts on itself through me. I am in a sense like a . . . like a magnifier. The world can use me to act on itself in amplified form.

'And this guide that's standing behind me is also that world, that universe. And as I realize that, he says, *"You've got it!!!"*

'And I hear kind of resounding, echoing, "The world is your guru."

'And then he says, "Sometimes it may be easier to talk to me than to the world." He says, "I'm behind you, and I'll always back you up." It's like he is the spirit of the world that's directly related to my power. And he says, "Yes, that's it."

'I ask him if he has a name.

'And he says, "Yes, I have many names."

'And then I say, "What can I call you?"

'And he says, "You can call me Peewee."

'And I say to him, "That sounds kind of strange!"

'And he says to me, "What would you like to call me?"

'And the words come to me something like Grandma, Grand Man, and then just a whole series of things that are takeoffs on that, one after another.

'And he says, "See?"

'And then after a while he whispers, "If you know me, it doesn't matter what you call me."

'And he's implying that naming is only for one little part of my being. There's one little part of my being that gets all concerned with naming, and names, and forgets names, gets all confused with words, and so on.

'And he says to me, "You've been trying to live out of a shoebox when you can have a castle as grand as the universe." He says, "If the universe is your castle, you're always at home. And if it's your castle, then you must care for it."

'And I tell him about all the plans I have and he says, "Yes, we're setting that up for you."

'And I ask him, "You and who?"

'And he says, "Me and the universe." He says, "We'll work with you. We're on your side."

'He says, "Tune in to me, and trust me."

[deep breathing]

'And then he says to me, "Are you ready to be transformed?"

'And I say, "Yes, I'm ready."

'And he does something to me, like he's squeezing something out of the front of me, I don't know what he's doing. And then it feels like when I breathe, after that, it feels like I'm breathing through those . . . through those . . . tubes, he says, "Just call them tubes." Ha, ha. I'm breathing through those tubes and also exhaling through them, like I'm just really clear in the middle and free and open, and I can breathe in directly all I want to breathe and also breathe out with no obstruction. [breathes deeply]

'It's a very clean, pure energy that he blows through them.

'And he says, "How do you feel?"

'And I say, "I feel good."

'And he says, "It's almost time to end this visualization."

'And I say to him, "Where will you go?"

'And he says, "Oh, I'll stay right here." He says, "I'll always be with you."

'There's something just really clear and clean about him.

[Robert sighs deeply]

'He said, "We have to grow you a tail." And I felt tremendous pressure on my tailbone, like something was sprouting out of it. A thick tail, almost like a kangaroo's tail, and it's both powerful and sensitive. And he says, "There, now you have 360 degree vision." And I see that it's like my ventral surface now folds around and extends up my back as the ventral surface of the tail. It feels very powerful and very springy, like I could spring on it like a . . . like a kangaroo does.

'And he asks me if I want to spring, and I say, "Well, I'm a little bit scared."

'And he says, "Just relax and bend your legs at the knees. Concentrate on your tail and let it snap you forward."

'I thank him very deeply with a beautiful gassho, and I get one back from him.'

Robert suddenly jumped out of the recliner with seemingly little effort. He was ecstatic.

Note:

1.   An aura, according to Robert Standard, is energy which emanates from the body. There are certain individuals who are capable of perceiving this energy and can use it in diagnosing illnesses and various energy states.

PART SIX

ENHANCING CREATIVITY

One of the most vital areas in which deep visualization can be used is in the generation and focusing of creative potential. Although this section exemplifies the use of visualization as an aid to writing, we have also used it successfully in music composition and the visual arts. In fact, from our experience visualizations can enhance any human activity.

17.

IN YOUR OWN WORDS

Dr John Stacey is a young man of many talents and a personal friend of ours who is Acting Director of a mental health centre. He reads voraciously and is interested in writing. In the following two visualizations, undertaken four days apart, he finds a guide who can aid him in his writing. The accounts were written by him from memory following each visualization.

17 July, 1981
'I sit in a comfortable old brown chair in the panelled or log-walled living room of a small cabin. The room is fairly dark, although a far side is quite bright, with sunlight from the brilliant day streaming in through the window. I hear a noise from upstairs, the sound of a person who is taking his time to come down and meet me. It is Gregory Bateson[1] and he is eyeing me intently, as he does throughout our talk, giving me the impression that he is seeing something, that he is seeing me. From the outset I sense a groundrule of honesty, seriousness of purpose, and intense engagement with each other, perhaps him with me more than me with him since he is keyed on me as I explore my thoughts. There is a spareness and elegance to his communications to me.

147

He talks about the need to simplify my living situation, to draw lines which are clear between my employment time and my time for personal work, to spend time silently in order to listen to what is important to me, and to carefully co-create a living space in which I will have the support and encouragement of others, the simplicity, and the peace necessary to start the process of self-expression through writing.

'Gregory Bateson says that I must not let my image of myself as a writer paralyse me and prevent me from writing as it has done so far. He says not to think of myself as a writer but to write. The only thing to do is to figure what is most important to me and then to talk about it in a way which makes it valuable and accessible to others.

'He tells me that the outdoors is very important to me, possibly as the setting for any writing which I will do. As far as a place is concerned, he says that I ought to live in a place that is very fruitful and green. The desert is a place to be awed, but it is not a place for me to be creative: British Columbia, Alaska, and the Applegate Valley came to mind.

'Guides assist action. Gregory Bateson will be there for me as I take this undertaking of writing seriously and begin my attempts. Bateson says to keep it simple at the start, with sketches, like this one of our talk. He says that the best writing is description, thorough, without redundancy. I see him as a mentor. I ask him about my father and my brother, and think that he is the same age as my father. He says that my father and my brother encumber me and that as long as I have needs for them I will not be free to act. Bateson's sternness underlines the sene of the imperatives of my nature and spirit, what I truly ought to do. He says that I ought to move, that I am too comfortable in my present home and that I need to have other persons around me who will provide support and encouragement. He says that I should surround myself with the best people and that I should put my extraversion and need for others to its best advantage by seeking to accept the influence of others whose vision is consonant with my own.'

21 July, 1981

'In my imagination there appears a painting, which I think is called *The Church at Anvers*. I am fighting the image a bit, but the church keeps coming closer. My guide, Gregory Bateson, is standing off to the right. He tells me to go into the church. I walk up a dirt path toward it, with Bateson following about twenty feet behind me. I am dressed in rough brown clothing, and I seem to be a pilgrim.

'The door to the church is open, and as I enter I am dazzled by the interior space of the church, by the stunning stained glass windows, by the hundreds of statues, and by the high ceiling, which, strangely enough, is a huge dome entirely made of stained glass.

'When I ask Gregory Bateson what the point is of my visiting the church he says to look, just look. As I look I get the feeling that I am witnessing the building of the church over a period of a couple of hundred years. Again I ask Bateson why I am here. He says that I must learn to see things as they are, and to see how things have come to be as they are. I realize, somehow, that I come from far away, and that I am to take this sight in fully and then return to my home town and tell, in my own words, what I have seen.

'It is time to go, and so Gregory Bateson and I leave the church. As I walk away from it, it becomes a painting once again, and then it becomes a painting on the wall in a museum. I recognize that the task before me is the same as Van Gogh's, to describe the church in his own "words", in his own idiom, to create one's own view of something real. I remember Bateson's telling me that the best writing is description, thorough, and through one's own eyes. He is going to come with me to my home town, to help me write about this.

'We camp for the night along the way, and as we sit beside the fire he says to me, "You are different from the others. The others will stay home while you will wander. You will see many things that others will not see, but you will come back and tell the others what you have seen, in your own words."

'When I ask if I will always be a wanderer, he looks down and says yes. Then he says that the writing will be the bond which connects me to others. It feels like a bond of love, the writing.

'I see my home town off in the distance. The scene looks like Norway, with steep mountainsides dropping off down into the head of a fjord, like Ardalstangen. The village is beautiful, with frame houses of many colours.

'We walk into the town and turn off to the left and go up a winding street. My house is on the left on one of the higher streets of the town. It is a blue house with white trim, and with two bay windows, one on each side of the front door. The reason for the two of them is to afford an excellent view of the town and the fjord and the mountains.

'When we enter the house we are met by a woman. At first I cannot tell whether she is a maid or my wife, but soon I recognize that she is my wife. She is dressed in a crisp blue striped dress and is wearing a white cap, and when she takes off the cap her long brown hair falls down beautifully. In some ways she is like Gregory Bateson, clear minded, getting things done, organized.

'She says to me lovingly and laughingly, "Now you get out of those clothes." I am aware of how the pilgrim's clothing is out of place in the house. She has prepared a bath for me upstairs, and so I go up and take a bath, while she stays downstairs and talks with Gregory Bateson. I can see that she really loves me. After I get out of the bath there are clothes for me, pants and shirt and a blue v-neck sweater.

'When I come downstairs, my wife and Gregory Bateson show me to a room, one of the front ones with the bay windows, which I will use for writing. It has a desk right by the window.

'Gregory Bateson is leaving now. He is staying down by the docks in a room. After he has left I go and sit with my wife. We have coffee and rolls. Bateson has told me to see him again when I have written this down.'

Note:

1.   It is not unusual to find an actual person as the guide, although in our experience it is uncommon. When it does occur it is usually someone greatly respected by the imager. In such situations the guide can have a powerful impact. I was doing a visualization once with a woman who held a very low opinion of herself, and the guide that she visualized was Jesus Christ. He said to her, "I created you, and I don't make junk! Show some respect for my creation!' On two or three occasions, I, myself, have been the guide envisioned. In such instances I am careful to use the term 'your guide' in continuing the visualization, rather than using my own name. It avoids complications, and it also helps the imager

differentiate between me as a person and the image that has come to them as their guide.

One general understanding I have come to is that if the imager is to get in touch with a quality they possess, such as their fear, or their power, or their ability to write, it is much better to visualize a manifestation of this quality rather than a guide. If, on the other hand, they are attempting to understand something external to them, such as another person, or a situation, etc., then a guide seems in order. I wouldn't hold to this generalization firm and fast, and there are certainly exceptions to it in this book.

18.

SAILING THE SEA

The two visualizations presented here were undertaken by Eligio Stephen Gallegos. The writing referred to in the visualizations is not the present volume, but the work on the territorial theory of personality which was mentioned in the Introduction.

9 September, 1981
'I find myself inside of a large egg, and there is someone with me who looks like a pirate, a magical pirate. Let me just be there for a while and see.

'He has a parrot on his shoulder. And a patch over one eye. The eye the patch is over can see, but it sees within. The patch is there so the eye will look within. He's just crackling with energy, like electrical energy. He's much bigger than I am. He has all of the appearance of a pirate, including a wooden leg, and yet within that appearance is a being which . . . the pirate is really just a guise in which this being appears. I ask him what his name is and he says Sinbad . . . he makes a play on the name, Sin Bad . . . and then he gives me another name, also in German . . . Glücklich.'

'What does that mean?'
'It means "happy".'

'I start to tell him why I've come to him and he interrupts me in the middle and says, "I know why you've come. There's something I need for you to take care of first." It's as if he knows what needs to happen.

'He's doing something to my face with his energy. Like he's beaming a stream of lightning into my face. It's crackling. And another beam into my heart, and another one down into my belly. Then my whole body's surrounded by crackling electricity and it's concentrated in those three areas. He tells me just to be there with him.

'He's sending me energy deep into my body rather than just on the surface. He says that my heart is the hardest thing to melt. He's concentrating on it. I have total trust in him. He tells me that I shouldn't invest him with such total trust; I should retain some of it for myself.

'He tells me that my head is jammed two foot down into my shoulders. Now he's aiming some of his energy at the base of my skull. All of this seems to be going on within this egg that we're in.

'He comes up and touches my chest and his hand goes all the way down into my body. He reaches way down deep, down into my feet, and says that he's straightening out things on the inside. He seems to be adjusting all kinds of stuff, muscles, bones, stretching things, indicating to me where things need more adjustment.

'It feels like he's simultaneously both pushing and pulling my lower vertebrae. He does something in the middle of my back and says it's bad. He seems to be coating it or wrapping it in some way. It feels like he's wrapping several vertebrae together so they'll hold as a unit while he adjusts the one above.

'Now he's moved up to my neck. He tells me that there are so many muscles and nerves in that area that unless they're all loose and each has enough of its own space, they will interfere with whatever energy needs to flow through them. Now he reached into my brain and grabbed a handle. [intense twisting] He tells me that I can't think flexibly unless my body is also flexible, and so I need to develop my body to be as flexible as possible. [much twisting] Now he's exerting some leverage at the base of my neck, from my neck down between my shoulders. [intense exertion]

'He stands back and says, "Okay, now we can talk." And then

he steps forward and says there's just one more minor adjustment. He sticks his hand in through my heart up into my right shoulder and grabs a handle in there that's similar to the one inside my face. He says okay.

'Now I tell him I need to talk about my writing, and he says, "First of all, get your office exactly the way you want it in order to be a writer. Set it up so that it's so comfortable that you just feel like writing." He tells me to have the particular books in there that I need, to feel the energy of all the pictures and rugs and icons, and to have it always available just for the writing. He tells me that I also need a place in there where I can be very silent, that the silence and the writing are complementary. In fact there are three activities he says, the silence, the writing, and then something else at the other desk which he says doesn't have a name. He says something like "gestation", or "creative seeding", come about as close to it as we can get in language.

'That room is to be like a womb in which the book can be born. He tells me that it's a very organic process. And that it's not too different from the division and specialization of cells and the creation of the embryo and development of the foetus.

'He says that the problem with writing is that you can only write one word at a time, whereas in the creation of the embryo the organs all get to a point where they develop simultaneously. But he says there is a similarity in the sense that the heart develops first, and eventually the nervous system, inner organs, skeleton, and so on. And that the infant isn't born until all the systems have gotten to a particular point where they're mutually self-sustaining, and that's the point at which the book has to arrive. But he says that the process will be very organic with me in the sense that I will work on whatever needs to be worked on at the time. And even when I'm not in the room the work will go on as if the room itself is an egg or a womb. And he says that is the significance of the egg in which we find ourselves. He assures me that I need to have the room exactly to my liking and to no one else's, even though to some people the room may look bizarre. He says the room is perfect for writing, even including the light, the wallpaper, and the curtains.

'He says I need to be ready to begin writing by next Monday, and that I have to be totally self-indulgent in the writing. It has top priority. He says that I'm not to confuse that with my responsibility to my wife or to my friends but that giving the book top priority is the way to be responsible to them.

'He tells me that the thing that needs to be of primary concern is the way I set up the room, the particular spirit, the spirit of writing, the spirit of creation. He tells me to go now with his blessing and be fruitful.

'I thank him for being with me and he tells me that he's there as much for himself as for me. And it feels then as if both of us dissolve through the eggshell.'

18 September, 1981

'I see a ship at sea. It's not a very large ship and the waves are fairly high. It's a choppy sea but not rough. It's a bright day, very nice sunshine, clear, a beautiful bright day. The water feels good, it feels energetic rather than rough. The ship is an old sailing ship with four masts, and heavily rigged. Its sails are down. Even though it's a sailing ship it doesnt seem like an old ship. It doesn't have the sense of age but of sprightliness.

'I don't see anyone on board, and I don't see me. There's just the ship bobbing up and down in the sea. Oh, up alongside of it now as I look further there's a very large ship, just mammoth, so that the sailing vessel looks like a little toy. In fact, I can only see the bow of the large ship. It's a very dark ship.

'There's something about the relationship between them . . . there's a reflection of the fact that my writing has a relationship to something bigger which I can't see, and which I may never be able to see. And now that I've understood that relationship it's like the big dark ship looms in the distance, in the background, and I am to keep that relationship in mind and go back to the sailing ship.

'I ask the sailing ship if it is my guide, and it says, "I am your vessel." I ask it what I am to do, and it says, "Board me." So I climb over the side on to it. The decks are beautifully varnished. The ship is beautifully clean, very pristine. It is bright, cheerful, happy. Like it's a brand new ship made in the old mould. The ship says to me, "I am your vessel," and I stand at the wheel and realize that I could steer it in any direction. The direction I steer it in is the same line, the same direction that the large ship is headed in. So that through reflection I can indicate some of the dimensions of the larger ship. And also by aiming it in the same direction I can indicate where the larger ship is headed.

'I tell the smaller ship, "I need to know about writing." And it answers, "Yes, that is what we're doing." It tells me that it is essentially my book, and that the function of my book is to illuminate something much larger, something with a direction of its own. The book is my vessel. The mistake I've been making is to think that the book is an endpoint in itself, rather than just a vehicle for indicating the outline of something much larger. The ship is happy with what I've said and smiles and nods to me, "Yes, that's the situation."

'The ship is indicating to me that I need to start this afternoon, and in one sense, I have to build that ship, in the sense of starting with the framing, starting to frame it, the ribbing, and all of that before it can sail. But that its sailing is not an end in itself, its sailing is for the purpose of illuminating something much larger, a much larger dimension and I have to keep that relationship very clearly in mind so I don't get ego involved.

'The ship tells me that the four sails are four elements in the book which will energize it. It tells me that what I am to do is to visualize it and imagine that I am on it, steering, and that the writing will come fluidly. It says that I'm in a good space for doing that, my energy is good, there's a sense of freedom. And also that I'm not to do things that sap my energy, that diminish my energy, but to keep my energy on an even keel.

'And I ask, "Okay, is that all? Can I go now?", and what it does in reply is to sail me to some land. I don't know if it's a continent or an island. The ship tells me that it doesn't matter since all bodies of land are connected at the centre. The whole earth is connected, is unified. If we only look at the surface of things then we tend to think of them as separate.

'I ask the ship what I am to do here on this land. It says, "Get off and go for a walk." And I find myself disembarking, climbing down a ladder on to the earth.

'On the earth is a bustling port, and I'm not to get too involved with that but just to walk wherever it feels right. So I leave the little village, it's a pretty little village, right at the edge of the sea, and I climb a mountain which has snow on top of it and looks

like an old volcano. Up at the top of the volcano I look down
into it, into the pit, and deep down inside I can see the red hot,
glowing molten lava. And I jump down inside.

'Then it feels like two things happen: the molten lava rises and
spews out in the shape of a beautiful flower, and I sink way down
into the centre of the earth. Down in the centre of the earth my
breathing becomes the breathing of the earth. And I just blend
and melt into the earth. The earth is alive, the world is alive.

'And I see it then, relative to the sky that it floats through. I
see it as this very alone little thing floating through the heavens,
but also in relation to something much larger that looms dimly
in the beyond, something massive. Something enormous, of which
the earth itself is only . . . something relative to which the earth
. . . the relationship between the earth and that thing is reflected
in the relationship between the sailing ship and the much larger
dark vessel. Like the earth is just an illuminator, an illuminant
of something enormous and unknown, something which can only
be indicated in terms of its being reflected by aspects of the earth.
And in that sense also, the earth is a bright happy place in the
same way that the ship was. There's just a deep dark massive
enormous unknown that is highly mysterious. And what we know
about the earth reflects that deeper element, as if the earth is a
reflection of the deeper element.

'And the boat then says, "Okay, you can go now."

'I feel myself deeply connected to that element, that enormous
element.'

19.

LEV

This visualization by Teresa Rennick was taken with respect to writing in general.

'The image comes immediately and in a somewhat confusing way. There is an orchard, an old one, with many trees containing various fruits and nuts. As soon as this image comes it is gone and I find myself inside a small frame house that is in the middle of the orchard. It was interesting looking at the trees, but suddenly I am just not there. I also didn't approach the house in any conventional way. Before I really see the outside of it, I am inside it. I have an idea of what it looks like but I have no memory of looking at it.

'I am inside the house immediately and standing in front of a table that is in the corner of a room. On the table is a cupcake that has a single lighted candle on it. I am focusing on what I have missed. I missed the walk into the house and I missed the walk across the room to the table. Now I am aware that I'm looking carefully at the table. It's a wooden table and I can't see the legs. They become very foggy and disappear before they reach the floor. The house seems to be totally empty except for me and the table and the cupcake.

'I'm not sure what to do. I came here to learn about writing but it seems a bit foolish to ask the cupcake. It's a white cupcake with pink frosting and a yellow candle. It's a conventional birthday candle but there is one difference: it doesn't seem to burn out with time. It stays long and lighted on the top.

'I say to the candle, "I want to find out about writing. Can you help me?"

'She seems to say, "Ask the table."

'My first inclination is to kneel down and look up under the table. I do this and examine how the table is put together. It seems usual in every way. It has four angling cross pieces in the corners to hold the legs in place. These are bolted on to the table. The table is small and rectangular. It is wooden and looks like it has been outside because the grain is rough and raised. It would pull apart at the centre so a leaf could fit but there is no leaf. There is a brass hook to hold the two sides of the table together but it is broken and not fastened. I look at the legs but I have a hard time focusing on them. I can't seem to focus on the legs and that seems important. I'm going to ask the table about the importance of the legs. It seems that the focus of the asking should be the little catch under the table that is broken.

'I ask but I am distracted before I can wait for an answer. And the distraction is the floor. It is a wooden floor with many knotholes. I particularly notice one knothole that is directly under the table next to a crack in the floor. This knothole makes quite a large opening. My fear is that a mouse or rat could very quickly come out of it so I am further distracted from listening for an answer to my question. I can't look away from the knothole.

'Suddenly a little mouse, a brown mouse, pokes his nose out of the knothole and looks at me. I ask if it is my guide or if it will take me to a guide to learn about writing. It looks like a curious little brown mouse. I usually don't like mice but I'm not afraid of this one. It has real bright black eyes that protrude from his head and a little pink nose with whiskers sticking out on either side of it. They are black and very alert-looking and give him sort of an amusing look.

'He doesn't listen to any questions I ask him but instead pops out of the hole and runs all over the room. He is very full of energy and runs up and down walls and over everything. I think he might be looking for something to eat.

'He just went back down the hole — his tail's black — and then he pops back up and says, "Come with me." I have this feeling of a genie being swept back into a bottle. My body feels almost liquid and feet first I am drawn downward into the knothole. I see as I go down why I had trouble with the table legs because they only go down about a third of the distance to the floor and then they disappear. They are either invisible or the table is levitating. I just notice this as I move through the knothole.

'There is just dirt, like a cave, under the house. The walls are made of dirt and rocks. I am small, just the same size as the mouse. It is dark down here. The mouse is friendly. He drapes one of his front legs around my shoulder and we walk deeper into the cave. I ask him what his name is and I'm not sure what he says. It is Levil or Levith, I don't quite understand. I ask him if he is my guide for writing and he says, "I have a few things I could show you." Since I can't understand his whole name he says I can just call him Lev. We continue to go downward although there is no stairway or passageway and it's hard to see ahead. He seems real social and he's still got his arm around me and he's just kind of . . . I can't really say what he's talking about but he's just kind of . . . making small talk or something. He bends his head and puts his face right over close to mine when he talks and just looks straight at me. He's quite intense. He has a sincere way of talking. I can't see where we're going, we're just ambling down. It's still dark.

'We've come to some doors. It's an arched doorway. It's got double doors. They're made out of real thick wood, and again it's wood that looks like it's been out in the rain all the time. The grain's really raised and it's not finished wood, it's substantial but it's quite weathered. There are two black porcelain knobs. The doors both open towards us. It feels like we're real deep in the earth. Now he's kind of quiet. We start to open the doors and he indicates I should be quiet.

'It's very bright in this room. It seems quite incongruous because I think it's a tent.

'It's high-ceilinged and there's a lot of gold and a big dome that goes up over the top of this white room and a lot of light is coming in. It's hard to say if it's windows or if it's just reflection. There are mirrors in the ceiling, and the floors are marble. And there are six . . . I don't know what they're called. There are six structures that are made out of granite, that are oblong, that contain . . . bodies. They're just . . . several feet apart from each other. There's a guard. It's a circular room, and the guard just walks. There's kind of a . . . the marble's a different colour along the whole outer edge of the room. It's like it's just suddenly different, light grey or something. And the guard walks around the perimeter of the room. He has a bayonet and he looks like one of the guards that guards the palace in England, he has a red coat and one of those real tall hats and a rifle with a bayonet over his shoulder. And he's marching stiffly around the room.

'Lev and I have to step back as he comes in front of us but he doesn't seem to notice; he just marches by. It's kind of hard to get used to the light.

'We cross over the path that the guard walks, we hurry across because he seems to go around pretty fast, and it seems like he would trample us if we were in his way. Lev and I are small compared to the guard. He might not even see us. We're the size of mice.

'It seems like our destination is to climb up . . . are they called mosques or what are they called? Those places where the dead lie. I don't know. Anyway, it seems like it's our destination to climb up these granite tombs and to look inside.

'And we climb up the first one and there's a little girl. And she has her hands . . . she has kind of long corkscrew curls, and she has her hands . . . folded over her chest, and she's got a lily in her hands. She's got on black patent leather shoes and a frilly dress. It's light green.

'And I ask her . . . she's dead but she can talk, I think. I ask her what I need to know about writing.

'It seems really simple, but she says, "Look at things like you did when you were a child." She doesn't even open her eyes, and I feel kind of reluctant to crawl back down but . . . I think I'll stay here a minute.

'Lev says that we need to move slowly in between the tombs. There's something about the movement between is as important as the . . . as the questions. I'm not sure what he means. It has something to do with absorbing.

'I climb up on to the next one. He climbs up too, although it's very high.

'Inside this one is a butterfly, and it's been mounted on a piece of white velvet. And the tomb is big, like it would be for a person, but all there is is a little butterfly. When I ask him what I should learn from him about writing, he says, "Avoid the impulsive flying away. When you are attracted to a flower, stay on the flower until you've learned what you need to learn."

'I've taken Lev's advice about going in between the tombs in a respectful way, and Lev and I have donned some very formal robes, like a minister or priest would wear when he's administering communion, or doing some kind of ceremony. Some sort of square hats. So it's like a little procession that we do, side by side, walking over to the next tomb.

'I . . . I can't see clearly what this is in the next tomb. My first impression is it's a puppy, but it looks like it's been . . . been harmed in some way. It seems like it's been mutilated, or . . . it's hard to tell what it is. It's lying there, it's got brown fur, and dried blood, and the limbs are kind of contorted in a strange way. It almost looks like it's a piece of fur that's nondescript. I couldn't even identify it.

'I ask the question. It says, "Pay attention to your feelings."

'Lev does some kind of thing, like he's pretending to be this priest and does this blessing over this animal. It's like he's kind of pompous but he's . . . but it's a joke.

'We're going counter-clockwise. We've done the tombs that were closest to the door. And now we're crossing a little corridor that's in the middle of the room. And the guard takes a sudden notion to come through the middle of the room, so we have to really hurry or he'll step on us. But again he doesn't notice us.

'We climb up to the next one and it's a nail. And I'm not sure if it's a big nail or a small nail because my size is so distorted. It could be a railroad spike or it could just be a regular nail, like you'd make a house out of. It seems to take up most of the tomb, but my size, it's . . . it's hard to say.

'I ask the nail what I need to learn from it about writing and he says, "Keep it simple, and useful."

'Lev is doing this funny thing now. We're at the foot of the tomb and he walks along balancing on his, on his . . . he walks on his hind feet all the time, but he's doing this balancing thing, and he's got some kind of cross or something in his hand and he's using it like a tightrope walker would use an umbrella.

'He's nice to be with. And then when he gets down, he's all . . . pomp and circumstancing, and very regal. He just marches ahead and I walk beside him to the next tomb.

'In the next tomb there's a very faded image of someone who is very, very old. And there's a cane that's lying there. It's like there was an old person there but they vanished or disintegrated. There's just the vaguest image of them being there. And all that's left is a wooden cane and very vague image.

'And so I ask the cane what I can learn from it about writing. And the cane says, "Listen to the old."

'This time between tombs, Lev is kind of like he's playing the part of absolutely no nonsense. He often puts his hand around my shoulder but this time it's like he's just very purposefully walking in a very direct way. Everything he does seems to be for some kind of effect and humour and he's walking very purposefully to the next tomb.

'This time instead of scurrying up on his own and letting me scurry up, he gives me a boost.

'There's a big watch in this one, a big pocket watch. I thought that it was going to tell me something about time, but what it does is the front becomes transparent and I can see the very intricate insides of the clock and he simply says to me, "Work."

'I feel a little reluctant to go, but Lev takes hold of my hand and just as fast as he can go, scurries down the tomb and he's just laughing, and I'm hurrying as fast as I can. He's much more sure footed on this granite that's absolutely vertical; he's just scurrying. And now he's running in and out with me through the legs of the guard, and the guard's still oblivious to us, but it's like it's a joke. And like we're running around the room three or four times and we pass the door and skid to a stop. It's like some kind of vaudeville act.

'There's something I'd like to know about the guard, and it seems to be what Lev is showing me by running in and out of his legs and making this whole thing so funny, and it's that the guard is absolutely ineffective at keeping us out, at keeping us stopped. It's like the guard can't interfere at all.

'We're done with it and so we just go towards the door and make a grand exit, opening both doors and just walking through it. And we come up through the knothole and come up into the house. The table is down on the floor now. It's not levitating; it's down on the floor. And I don't know what the cupcake's doing. It's still there.'

'Ask Lev.'

'He says it was just a little ruse, a little technique to draw me to it, to get me pointed in the right direction. He thought it would attract me. It has no meaning. Anyway, I'm still small, and the table's very low to the ground and so we just climb up on the table, blow out the candle, and eat the cake.

'I like him alot.

'Oh, we hug and hug in parting. It's like one of those scenes from the old movies, in saying goodbye, and we're over-dramatizing it, just hug and then part a little bit, and hug again and part a little bit, walk to the edge of the table and then come running back and hug. He's so funny.

'Finally I'm ready to go and he's under the table. The table is only a little ways off the ground and so I can see his nose out of the knothole and he waves a white handkerchief, and I tell him goodbye and thank you. And I'm ready to come back.'

PART SEVEN

THE BOOK

20.

BLACK ELK

'Take a deep breath and let your eyes close. Feel the contact that your body makes with the floor, and the support that the floor provides. Imagine that your body is growing roots, way down deep into the earth . . . way down, and that the soil is deeply rich, beautifully moist, thoroughly nourishing. Let your entire body relax down into the roots. Let yourself be nurtured by the roots. The earth provides completely.

'And as you become aware of the rhythm of your breathing, imagine that you're breathing in the sky and the sunshine, and that it is brilliantly renewing, that it renews every cell in your being, including the roots.

'Imagine also that as you exhale you're letting go of everything you no longer need.

'Allow your mind to be beautifully peaceful and still, very, very settled, magnificently at peace.

'Allow there to be in your imagination now, an opening, a clearing, a place where you can go in order to meet your inner author. Just let that place appear to you. When you begin to see it, describe what it looks like.'

'First of all, as I let my roots grow very deep, I'm aware that they look like ginseng roots. They have a wonderful capacity of anchoring me, and of being very old and thick and substantial. They also have the quality of being legs and of being mobile. So I have the feeling that I am incredibly anchored but I could go anywhere.

'And when I'm taking in breaths of sky, it seems that usually I have a feeling like it's blue sky and very clear, but today I have a feeling more of the sunlight. So as I take in breaths it feels like everything above me is a golden, beautiful bright colour.

'And I'm aware immediately when I clear a space that the space is in my abdomen, around my navel, and there is somehow a connection between that part of me and my head. And it seems that I'm the landscape and the space . . . I'm just below the surface . . . and the space where this little house appears that I see is just right above my abdomen.

'The house is a house I've seen before. It's white and it's very, very small, just one room. And it's very rustic in some ways and very well kept in some ways. It's made with narrow horizontal siding and has a wooden shingle roof. From the outside you can see that there's a fireplace or a wood stove. There's a chimney on one side. It's very tiny. It's got a porch on one side with a wooden railing, and steps that lead up to the porch.

'I've seen it before. I've visited it before. It's on the grounds where John Neihardt lived and did his writing. It's in . . . I can't think of the name of the town; it's in Nebraska. I want to say Laurel but I don't think that's it. I just don't remember. I visited it a long time ago and this little house is where he did his writing. And it was some distance from the main house.

'On the inside it has a wooden table and a typewriter and a fireplace. It's very simple. It almost seems unpainted on the inside. Very white on the outside and unpainted on the inside. It's not shabby, it's just like there was no need for decoration and so it was left plain. There's a rocking chair on the porch and windows on all sides of the house.

'I have a sense of ghosts, like how it was a long time ago.'

'Is your inner author a ghost?'

'It seems . . . uh, I can see it there. I'm standing in the doorway and I just barely, barely see an outline, a body sitting at the typewriter. I ask, "Are you my inner author?" and I can hardly see. I can't tell if it's male or female, its so vague, but it types out, "Yes." Now I see it clearly. It's kind of interesting . . . I ask, "What is your name?" and it types out "I'm John Neihardt." It's kind of interesting because I've never even read a book he's written. I tell him that and he says . . . no, he types out . . . he types out everything instead of speaking. I said, "I haven't even read a book. I bought a book and I've only read part of it." And he says, "That's all right. You may someday but there's no need."

'It feels like I have a number of things that I could talk about or quite a few things I could ask, and I'm not exactly sure how to go about it.'

'Why don't you ask him?'

'Okay.

'I say to him that I have a number of things that I could ask, but that I'd primarily like to know about the book that you and I are working on . . . let's see . . . I'm looking at the typewriter and it says, "You have begun," but I'm distracted because right behind him there is another ghost and it's Black Elk. I see the relationship between what I'm doing in writing and what John Neihardt is doing in . . . uh . . . it's like if I could describe the scene, it would be Black Elk standing right behind John Neihardt, and John Neihardt is doing the typing but the book is coming from Black Elk. I can see from that relationship that it's important to know that I'm the vehicle, and that there's this vast, ageless wealth that's directly behind me and that I have contact with. And if I'm very clear and allow it the book will come through me.'

'Do you think you should talk to Black Elk? Ask him if he can talk to you.'

'I can try that.

'I . . . he doesn't talk to me in words, but I ask him what I can learn from him and he says, "You can learn everything." I see him standing there. He's standing on the floor of this small house. I have a sense of how he is connected with every aspect of . . . of . . . it's like I see his feet very firmly planted on the earth and he's in connection with the sky and the clouds and inside himself, and I get a feeling of trust, or faith, something like that. Almost like he's just absolutely a ghost, he's just . . . like I can see that he's an Indian dressed in the old way, and when I look at him I see everything.

'Um, I, I, I, have this awareness of another ghost in the room. It's a woman, and it's John Neihardt's wife. She's a sculptress and my feeling is she also is capable of . . . the scene is she's a ghost, too, and she's kneeling on the ground and she's making a statue. I can't see what it is but I have the feeling that she is also allowing, well, it's like the universe, or whatever Black Elk represents, to come through her and make the sculpture, and my awareness is that the energy is the same . . . there's something about them all being ghosts, which helps me see it, there's nothing to stop the . . . Black Elk's spirit from going directly through them, and the result being the creativity, whether it's the words on paper, or whether it's the sculpture. And . . . let's see . . .

'I have an image of myself with the spirit of Black Elk directly behind me, and then a clearness which is necessary for . . . for the process to happen.

'It's almost like there's . . . I'm seeing John Neihardt again at the typewriter and he takes the paper out and is holding it up toward the sky, looking at it with his arms outstretched, and it feels like there's some . . . there's some sense of what he's writing not belonging to him personally. It's like there's something freeing about the writing coming from such a deep place that it no longer . . . well, there's something not miserly about it, it's like . . . it's something like . . . I understand it but I don't know how to describe it. I see him with his hands upraised with the paper and the words he's written but that have come from this incredible spirit, and there's something about him not owning it and not . . . it's his but it has . . . well, I can't describe it, it's just something not describable. As he holds his paper up I can feel the incredible depth behind him. He's looking up at the paper and it's almost like he's beyond being judged for it because it's more than he is; it's deeper than he is.

'I ask, "Do you think the book will be successful?" and it's almost like that's a dumb question. It's not an important question, somehow; it's funny. But he looks over his shoulder and I'm aware of Black Elk behind him . . . it seems like . . . you know, it's like there's just . . . this amazing feeling of the spirit that I have that . . . I have that feeling of . . . how that spirit surrounds the book.'

'Do you want to ask either one of them if they have some advice they want to give you?'

'All right.

'Ohhh. I ask Black Elk and he said, "You need so much reminding about what I've shown you about trusting." And I see that's true, and it makes me, oh . . . it seems like . . . I feel . . . cradled, or . . . held in that feeling.

'I ask John Neihardt and he shows me that he has a full waste-basket; it's full of crumpled-up paper, and he says, "I've written a lot of very bad things but nothing is wasted." And I see that that's true, that . . . that I'll write about a lot of things, but it's not wasted. Because I have so much to learn.

'I ask Mrs Neihardt, too. And she says, "Remember that this expression all has the same result, and try many different ways of expressing, because the expression is what you need. Expressing yourself in one area will enhance expressing yourself in another area."

'I feel like I'm ready to go, and then the thought occurs that you could ask something, Steve.'

'Would you ask John Neihardt if he can give me a sense of the overall book?'

'All right.

'He's just looking at it with me while I look at it in the way that you have it in your den, and it's almost like he's affirming the way he sees it. He's nodding . . . he's saying, "The way this is laid out has spirit, and continue to keep that in mind." He doesn't have suggestions for major changes. As he looks at it I feel that old spirit that surrounds it, how it's evolved with that in mind, and is right. I ask him what the name is and he shows me the outside of the book with the cover and I can't read the name. On the back is a picture of you and me together, a casual picture; I see that clearly. But I can't read the name on the front. He says, "Steve's inner guide knows the name." Ha, ha, ha. Oh, how interesting. It seems like that's the sense . . . like I'm the back, I'm somehow underneath the book, and you're the front, and that seems right. Do you have any more questions, Steve?'

'No, I don't.'

'Black Elk is there, always Black Elk is behind him, or behind Mrs Neihardt, or behind me, and my sense is when I finish with the visualization Black Elk will stay with me like that's the thing I . . . that's the trust and cradling that I need.

[pause]

'Oh, I say, "Isn't it funny that I still don't remember the name of the town in Nebraska where your house is?", and he says, "We're really not there." It's funny, because that's my sense, too.'

'Thank them for being with you and also thank them for me.'

'All right.

'It seems like Mrs Neihardt, especially, acknowledges the thanks from you. Now I see you kneeling next to her and Black Elk is behind you both, and you both are working on the same sculpture; I can see your hands so clearly, Steve. She says that you should listen to the advice that she gave me.'

'Tell her I will.'

'I tell them both thank you, and Black Elk was . . . it's almost like . . . he's beyond thanking, he's just . . . I'm going to bring him back with me.'

21.

AHAB THE ARAB

'Make yourself really comfortable in whatever way is necessary so that you feel your body able to really relax. And become aware of the contact that your body makes with the floor. And wherever your body makes contact with the floor, feel roots growing from it. And feel the roots growing very deeply into the earth. And look at the roots while they grow, how thick, how strong, as they grow deeply into the earth.

'Become aware that you are taking in deep breaths of fresh air. Feel the air swirl around in your body and then go deeply into the earth, through the roots. Swirling through your whole body, and as you exhale let the air bring with it anything that is old, anything that is unneeded, and just let go of it into the air. And bring in what is fresh and new into your body.

'When you're ready, clear a place in your imagination where you can go to meet your inner author, or to meet a guide to tell you about the book on visualization, and tell me when you're there.

'Yeah, the space that I see is like a tent, like a white tent. It's kind of a blank thing, and it's like an arabs' tent that has a number of peaks inside of it, very large, canvas spread over a number of tent poles of varying heights. So that it's almost like a work of art.

'I see it out in the desert. It's a white tent, very sandy desert, like the Sahara. And there are camels around and some people on the camels. And I'm up to the door of the tent, now.

'There's a little string of bells, camel bells, tied to the tent. I give it a shake and it jingles melodiously, very harmoniously. A dark man in a turban comes to the door, and he feels slightly effeminate. Very sensitive eyes, very large, sensitive eyes. He's very slight, very slim, and moves in a very feminine manner. He has very pronounced teeth, a slight stubble of a beard; he's slightly gaunt. And he's slightly dirty, too.

'I ask him if he's my guide, and he says, "No, come in." He lets me know that he's the, kind of like a servant or a butler. Kind of like a manservant. And he holds the door open and I walk in.

'Inside the tent it's very luminous, because it's white and there's a bright sun outside. So it's very luminous inside. And there are oriental rugs all over, on the floor, on the sand, hanging on the inside walls. Some of them are forming some partitions. They're very colourful; they're very beautiful rugs. It's very richly appointed.

'There's a small room that is set off with oriental rugs for walls, and I feel that who I'm supposed to meet is in there. And indeed, the manservant ushers me over there and there is a gap at the ends of the rugs; there's an opening, and I bow my head and go through the opening.

'Inside there is a man who is very fat, very jolly, and very rich, very worldly, full of worldly experiences, very relaxed, very settled. And his eyes are heavily lidded. He has very fat jowls. He also has a turban on but it's a multi-coloured turban. And he's sitting up on a mound that could either be a heap of rugs or a heap of sand covered with rugs. But he's sitting on top of this mound toward the back of the little room.

'I go up and I bow to him and I ask him is he my guide; is he the author within.'

'What's his name?'

'I ask him what I can call him and he says "Ahab the Arab."

'He says, "I am a story teller, and I come from a long line of story tellers."

'It's a tradition in his family. It goes way, way back. It's been both inherited and handed down from one generation to the next. And he's the current generation.

'And I tell him I'm writing a book, and he says, "Oh, yes. Tell me about it."

'I tell him it's a book of visualizations, about visualizations in therapy and growing. He says, "Oh, yes. You want to take people into the magical realm. That is a land that few people know about. And you want to open the doors wide for them." And he says, "You want to know that most will not understand. But there will be a few for whom this will be a vital work, vital to their growth." And he says, "Don't think in terms of the present generation. Think in terms of people years from now, who are not yet born, and whose eyes will be opened by your book. Don't limit yourself to what is current. See broadly and deeply, and recognize that you are writing it for people that you will never know and whose worlds you will never know, and this is still a doorway for them."

'He says, "Write it as if it were a magical book. You don't need to say that but you can have that understanding. Since most people won't understand it anyway, you may as well go deep for those that will. Don't worry too much about what editors might think of it. If it's to be published it will be published. You're not writing it for editors. You're writing it for those people in the future, and they will appreciate your consideration." '

'I tell him I need some help in structuring and sequencing the book, the chapters of the book.

'He says, "Sit down here with me and I'll show you something."

'I have no idea what he's going to show me.

'He has a book there which is a very old, handwritten book, with illuminated pages, and written in beautiful calligraphy. It's written on parchment.

'He shows me how even the very first page has a beautiful illumination on it, a beautiful picture. He's indicating to me that the picture can be glanced at, or you can go into it very, very deeply. That you can just look at it on the surface or you can look at it in another dimension which goes deep and is endlessly deep.

'He says, "Realize that each of your chapters will be like this. They are like your paintings where people will see things in them which you yourself have never seen. So you can't be too concerned about how people might see them, since that is something you may never know."

'On the first pages there is a little illumination on the left which is about the height of the page, and then there is some calligraphic writing and I don't know what it says. And he says, "This is a picture that complements the story."

'And then he flips through the pages and as he progresses on through the book, the pictures get larger and larger and the story gets shorter and shorter. Not that the story is lacking, but the story is almost like a code, precisely articulated, and compact. But since the pictures are ultimately indescribable, you could talk about them forever. The stories, the book as you go through it gets deeper and deeper, as you work your way through it. Until the final pages are nothing but pictures. And maybe a word, or an exclamation point, or something of that nature, accompanying them.

'And he says, "See your book in this way. The first chapters will be well described and as you work your way through the book the description needs to be less and less and the visualizations themselves predominate. So, judging each chapter against every other, you'll have no trouble aligning them in this sequence. This way also you'll draw in those people that are very dependent on description. You may not wake many people up, but you will wake up a few."

'I ask him about money, and he says, "The book itself is wealth. Don't be too concerned initially. The main thing is to get it published and over time," and he indicates like maybe over fifty years, "Over time the book will enrich you. And having published this, then you can publish others."

'He says, "You might also think of a book on art therapy down the road. Each book you publish can be an introduction to the next, so that the sequence will be natural and organic."

'I ask him how many chapters it should have, and he says, "Twenty-one chapters in seven sections. Two to four chapters per section. Again, the sections will make themselves known to you. The more elementary ones at the beginning and the more magical ones at the end. This book will leave those people that it touches hungry for more."

'He says, "You may decide to work only with creative people, rather than with people with problems."

'I tell him that the situation here feels kind of nebulous to me, kind of shimmering, and he says, "Yes. It's the heat." It's almost like it's unstable, it's floating around, it's not cloudy but more like the situation here is a hologram, and he takes me down through a hole which is in the top of the mound on which he's sitting. It's like an ant hole, but it's large. We go into it and there's steps leading down. The walls are of earth, there are some little roots sticking our here and there, the walls are adorned with hangings and with oriental carpets. It's lit by torches and it goes down at a fairly steep angle. He leads me down it and we each carry a torch.

'As we get down in it it's very cool. And we get down to a place where there is an underground stream, and shortly before we get there the tunnel itself is lined with some kind of brick, large brick. And then we get down to where the stream is running and that's all tunnelled out also. The water in the stream is very pure and he dips a cup, a cup that could be gold or brass or copper that is enamelled, a cloisonne cup, into the water, and the water is very cool and clear and pure, and he hands me a cup of it and I drink it. And it feels like it enters my bloodstream immediately. It courses through my body and cools me with a shudder, but it also clarifies my whole body. Like that coolness is just a brilliant clarity that courses through my body. And anything that is an impediment, or anything that is not aligned, anything that is improper in my body, immediately becomes very evident. I become very aware of it. Everything that is balanced becomes totally clear, like I could see right through it. But anything that's unbalanced becomes heavy and very noticeable. And I feel it in both arms, my left arm from my shoulder on down and my right arm from my elbow on down, I feel it in my right leg, and in the middle of my back. And the story teller, Ahab, comes up to me then, and cuts off all these parts, my left arm at the shoulder, my right arm at the elbow, my right leg at the hip, including the hip, and a round piece in the middle of my back, and throws these all into that underground stream. And when they hit the water they turn into strange animals. Strange animals that are a bit indistinct and very colourful. There's an alligator there with very red lips, and a blue-green shimmering skin, and it seems to be made out of my left arm, what my left arm turned into. And there's something sly and cunning about it. Something kind of deceptive.

'My right arm turns into something that looks like a weasel, white, maybe ermine. And it can swim. And it's very sleek. But it's not very large and it's not very strong. But it's quick.

'My right leg turns into a hippopotamus that's wearing a skirt. And it's blue and has long eyelashes. It's feminine. And it's very lazy and very shy. But it's big and lumbersome.

'The part of my back turns into something that looks like a moth, or a butterfly. It's big. And it seems to have both the characteristics of a moth and of a butterfly. On the one hand it's kind of nondescript, just a greyish brown, and on the other hand it has some definite patterns in it which are black and brownish yellow.

'Then I ask him, "What do these things mean?"

'And he says to me, "Talk to them and find out."

'So I decide to talk to the white ermine first. And I ask it, "What is your name?" and it says, "My name is Herman." [laughter] And I say to it, "I don't understand your relationship to my arm." And he says, "Watch me." And he darts around quickly and in darting around he's so fast that he creates some beautiful patterns. Even though he's white the patterns are multi-coloured, in soft tones, like pastels. Geometrical figures, but figures that seem to have some depth. It's like his own whiteness gives a beautiful luminosity to them. And he does this very naturally, very instinctually. I understand from this that my right arm is the artist, and that I have not given it the freedom that it needs. It's like I have subordinated it to my self and I need to give it the freedom that it needs to create what it needs to create, to draw, to paint, or whatever. It's like I've made it very lonely, very isolated. I've limited it tremendously. I have not allowed it the richness that is its right. And I say to Herman, "Do you have anything else to tell me?" And he says, "Watch." And he dives straight into the stream and burrows a hole way down deep, really deep, right down to the centre of the earth. And then he comes back up, immediately pops up into the air out of that hole and says, "See?" And I understand from that that my right arm is capable of remarkable depth, and that its natural process is in art and in things with beautiful depth. It instinctively goes in those two directions. And I say to Herman, "Anything else?" And he says, "Nope." I thank him then, and he reattaches himself to me at the elbow but remains the ermine. It's a beautiful gift.

'I look at the other animals, the other three, and kind of weigh them, and I realize that I need to talk to the butterfly last, so it's a choice between the hippopotamus and the alligator. I realize that I need to go with the alligator first to keep things balanced.

'And I say to the alligator, "What do you need to tell me? I don't understand the relationship between you and my left arm." It has lips that are bright red, almost like they have lipstick on them but they don't, and it gives me a sickening sweet smile. There's something sly and manipulative about the smile. I say to it, "I get the feeling that I can't really trust you." And it chuckles way down deep inside. I see now how overly friendly it is, almost sickeningly friendly. And at the same time I see those very sharp teeth, just razor-like. And it says to me, "You get the point?" I see its remarkable subtlety and, you know, like it's covering up a great viciousness. And I understand that this is something I have done all my life. I have tried to cover over my own viciousness with a sickening sweetness. But what I see anew here is that I have always thought that was very central to me, and I see now it was just an aspect of me. I had identified with that and I see it's something somewhat peripheral. And I also see the complementation between that and my artistic right arm.

'I say to it, "You're pretty sly, aren't you?" and it says, "Yes, and I always tell the truth." And a fiendish laugh comes out of it. Like even when it's telling the truth it's lying.

'I say to it, "Tell me about your skin." It has this shimmering skin, a beautiful blue but almost like oil on water, almost metallic in some way. I really can't get ahold of its colour, it's made up of so many subtle different colours. Its overall appearance is a bluish sheen, but if you look closely there's white, there's red, there's yellow, there's green, there's black, there's blue. Very deep shades. Almost like one of the pointillist's paintings.

'And I see that it's full of paradox. It's an animal that is difficult to get ahold of, difficult to understand, because it's so full of opposites. And it's like there needs to be some kind of resolution between the sharpness of those teeth and the sweetness of the smile. Like they're both extreme. The viciousness and the sickening sweetness are both extremes and they need to somehow integrate themselves into something that's more balanced. They're both polarities; both exist as polarities. And they both need to let themselves melt together into something that is more in the middle.

'The alligator's going through some kind of strange gyrations now, almost like it's going crazy. And I see some teeth that are not sharp, they're very flat bottomed and very rounded where they go into the gum. They look very much like the teeth of a boyhood friend of mine who committed suicide. And I start seeing how much anger there is in those teeth. And how that conflicts with the need to be liked, to be loved, which is what produces that sickening smile.

'It feels like the alligator is really tormented. Tormented by that tremendous division in this opposition. And like it's a very primitive kind of thing. A thing that is a limbic function: love and hate, the need to be nurtured and yet the tremendous anger.

'And I say to it, "How can I help you resolve this great difference, this great division?"

'And it says to me, "Put me on."

'So I pull it on over my head as if it were a costume or a skin. My arms pop out its little stubby legs, my legs fit into its hind legs and I feel the big, powerful tail. And the legs are just splat out to the sides. So that it really crawls on its belly and pushes and pulls itself along with the legs. It doesn't hoist itself off the ground.

'I feel that tremendously long snout and those vicious teeth. And the eyes that are very expressionless, and yet can see almost everything around. That sickening smile is so extreme that it pulls back the lips, which is what makes them so pronounced. That is also what makes the teeth so pronounced. It's like the sickening sweetness *is* the thing that makes it so vicious, *is* the thing that emphasizes its viciousness.

'And it says, "If you wouldn't try to accommodate people so much, you wouldn't get so angry."

'I bend over backwards, I go overboard to do whatever people want me to do and doing that is what makes me so angry because there is nothing of me left for myself. As a child I was forced to do that with my parents, particularly my father. And the anger is an anger of that attitude being forced on me. It's almost like a rubber band being held very taut; if you let go of one end it snaps to the other. What if you let go of both ends?

'I feel the rubber band being let go of at both ends and then it jumps around, it keeps jumping around at the centre. And it is alive. The rubber band itself seems to be my lips, but jumping around in the centre they're very relaxed, they're no longer pulled back so taut that they expose those vicious teeth. And when that rubber band jumps around in the centre, relaxed and loose, then the teeth become rounded and soft rather than sharp and razorlike.

'And suddenly the whole alligator seems to be made of rubber, a soft, flexible latex, really relaxed. And now it jumps around like the rubber band. Playful. Oh, I see what's in the centre of those two extremes, now! Is play! My father never allowed me to play with him! He was always extremely severe! There was never any playfulness with him as I was growing up.

'The alligator's now a big rubber toy. A play toy that you would float in the water when you take a bath. It's friendly and playful. And it can wad itself up into a ball that can bounce. And stretch itself into a slingshot. And it says to me then, "You see?" And I say, "Yes, I see."

'It comes up to me and attaches itself to my shoulder. It is there now as a flexible alligator like a child's toy, but it could still become vicious or overly friendly. At extremes. But those extremes are very seldom. It's just that in my childhood those extremes were the usual case in my relation to my father.

'So I now have an ermine for my right arm and a rubber alligator for my left.

[deep breath]

'Wow! It's almost like I need a rest before I can go talk to the hippopotamus. I just realized the play on words there: the hippopotamus. [breathes deeply]

'Oh, my jaw just feels . . . Uh! Wow, feels like it's finally relaxing after having been tight all my life. It feels like now I'll be able to talk! That sickening sweet smile and those vicious teeth, the strain between them kept me from talking, and from being playful, verbally playful. That's closely related to me seeing that pun on hippopotamus. Uh. It's almost like it goes deep into the bone, even, of my jaw, my chin, my teeth. [deep breath] Oh. Mmmmmm. Oh. Whew.

'And there's some indication that I need to go to the butterfly first, before I go to the hippopotamus.

'So I go to the butterfly, then. Maybe just because I sense that the hippopotamus will be so heavy that I need some kind of lightness between the alligator and the hippopotamus. I go to the butterfly. It's a big butterfly, yellow and black, kind of a yellowish brown and black. A lot of black. The black forms the patterns.

'I go to the butterfly and I say, "I don't know what you were doing in my back."

'And it says, "I'm the yellow streak that was down your back."

'It says, "I'm what kept the alligator smiling, rather than it just lashing out. I am your cowardice. And you're lucky you had me, because if you hadn't you would have been more destructive. You've always looked down on me, but I'm really your salvation. Nothing goes to waste. The alligator is now your strength, your beautiful, playful strength. And I am your caution. I was your caution carried to extreme, but that's because the circumstances were extreme. You always looked down on me but I saved you."

'I'm very aware that it also formed a shield on the back of my heart.

'And it says, "Yes, I shielded you from situations you would've gotten into which would've been very painful for you. I'm your protector."

'It shows me that there's not only yellow in it but also black, deep black, jet black. In a beautiful pattern. And when these melt together, when these are blended together, what results is the brown, soft moth. The moth is very unnoticeable. It's the colour of sand. It's also very fuzzy. There's a beautiful softness to it. So it's like if I lived in a normal environment, if I'd grown up in a normal environment, it would've remained just a very soft, brown moth, that would flutter here and there. But because of the extreme situation it turned into that jet black and yellow butterfly.

'I ask it if it has anything more to tell me, and it says no, for me to put it back. To put it back in my back. And to remember that it's there, even though it's colourless. Even though it's very unnoticeable. And though people don't pay much attention to a moth, for me to remember that it's true.

'So I put it back there and it covers my whole back now. Before it only covered the centre spot. The wings are the sides of my back, its body is my spinal cord, and it's bent just like my back is bent. And that's how it had its close relationship to my left arm. To the alligator.

'There's something very soft about my back, now, rather than intense. The black was an intense anger, and the yellow was an extreme cowardice. It's like they've melted together now and they've become that moth, a soft moth. Again, the moth is middle ground, just like the rubber band was middle ground, like play was middle ground.

'I see that the antennae of the moth are my ears. And it's like my ears become hyper-aware with the moth back in place. But not in a vigilant way. In a very soft way. Like my hearing takes on some new contours, very soft contours, but like my hearing is right there doing . . . contouring whatever it is that I hear.

'And it feels like there's a new richness in my cheeks, a result of my ears opening up. It's like before my ears were very vigilant, and they would only hear things that were very scary or that would provoke my anger. It's like now I'm capable of hearing all kinds of softness. [deep breath]

'And I go up to the hippopotamus now. It has a skirt on and has long eyelashes. It's a stuffed hippopotamus that is blue. It's a hideous animal. It's great big. A child's toy.

'I go up to the hippopotamus and I ask it what its relationship is to my right leg, from the hip on down. And it giggles and waves its long eyelashes at me. It has a really big ass. And it's gentle, very gentle for being such a big animal. I ask it again, and again it just waves its eyelashes at me.

'I ask if it could talk to me, and there are two things: one is a growl like a lion that comes out of it, and the other is a meow like a cat, like a kitten. And so I understand that it, also, is two extremes. And I know that it has to do with my mother, and maybe my relationship to women.

'Ohhhh. It's like it's an animal. A cat. A feline. And it has been turned into this . . . this hideous toy, this hideous stuffed animal. It's insulated! The stuffing insulates that lion, that feline that's in it, which has a range all the way from a kitten to a ferocious lion.

'It's like my mother imposed on me a . . . kind of . . . covered me, part of me . . . took a part of me and covered me over like a toy. Insulated it. Made out of it a hideous toy rather than allowing it its natural sleekness, its natural jungleness, its natural . . . its natural organicity.

'I understand it has to do also with my sexuality. Like my sexuality was very animal-like, and she tried to pad that over with something that didn't fit at all.

'She took a part of me that is naturally feline, naturally graceful, which has the movements of a cat, and turned it into this hideous stuffed hippopotamus.

'I say to the hippopotamus, "What do we need to do?" And I hear this roar of the lion inside and I know that I have to take off this . . . this upholstery. So I take a seam in the hippopotamus and I . . . I just pull the thread all the way back, like a zipper. And out of it comes a lion, full maned, and it shakes off the cotton that's been stuffed around it, almost suffocating it. Shakes it off and pulls itself out of the inside of the hippopotamus. What's been done to it is a tremendous travesty.

'It's not a vicious lion. It's a powerful lion, but it's not necessarily vicious. It could be, depending on circumstances. And it sits there, lies there, very serenely licking its paws, washing itself, cleaning off all the cotton, some of which still sticks to it. It's a remarkable noble animal. It has an inherent nobility. And the nobility didn't diminish because of what was done to it. But now it's extricating itself from this . . . this hideous thing that's been done to it, cleaning itself up, standing, shaking itself off, stretching. It's been all cramped up in there. It's been almost unable to move. It's been in a straitjacket, unable to feel, unable to move, it could only growl occasionally.

'It's like my mother took my felinity and tried to cover it, hide it, insulate it, turn it into something totally its opposite, a stuffed toy.

'Now I understand! The butterfly had to turn back into a moth before the lion could be freed.

'The lion is very accepting, it's not even indignant. It's just out and so now it's out. It seems there is not even anything I could say to it. I try to hug it and it's just kind of there. It seems like it's its own domain, and it's not to be influenced by . . . by appreciativeness, or by confinement, or whatever. It's not diminished, nor is it augmented, by anything.

'It finishes cleaning itself off and then it goes and drinks from that stream, that underground stream. It gets into the water, soaks a little, gets out, shakes itself off. Cleaning itself. It's a naturally clean animal.

'And the stream carries the stuffing and the fabric of the hippopotamus away.

'The lion is totally courageous, totally noble, totally unflappable, imperturbable. Yawns and just sits there, looks around.

'Then it gets up and stands on its hind legs in front of me, stretches its arms out and merges with me. [deep breath]

'And I understand that I am to bathe in that stream now. I get into it and I lie down, let the water course over my body. I lie down feet first, feet against the current. And then I move so that my head's against the current. I roll over in it. Like it's washing me clean. And then I get out and I shake like the lion. And I feel very . . . very rosy, very jolly, very alive. My skin's just tingling. Very refreshed. Remarkably invigorated. [deep breath]

'And sometimes I see myself as me and sometimes I see myself as the lion. Like they're interchangeable. And it might even be more realistic to see myself as the lion.

'I look at Ahab and he's sitting up on a little mound of earth. He looks at me deeply, and says, "See. I told you that this was a magical book. You've just written the last chapter."

'Then he and I go arm in arm back up the stairs and the spirits of those animals come along behind, like they're my guardians in a way: the ermine, the moth, the rubber alligator . . . and the noble lion. Proud and noble. Not proud, really, it's like an inherent integrity. Like pride can be challenged, but the lion really can't be challenged.

'And we come up inside of the tent once again. Ahab covers the opening with his rugs, and sits on them again.

'He says, "Come back and see me again, before you send the book to a publisher."

'I say, "I will. Thank you for all of this."

'He makes a gesture as if to say, "That was nothing."

'As I exit, his manservant is waiting for me and ushers me to the door of the tent. As I step outside the manservant unrolls a small carpet and I get on it. It whisks me away through the sky, very high. I can see the desert down below, and then the ocean. And it carries me across the American continent, and there's our city down below. It circles around, counter-clockwise, and then lands.'

INDEX

anger, 17, 39, 54, 64, 65
archetypal psychology, 15
archetypes, 14
Aristotle, 12
art, 13
aura readings, 136

Bosch, H., 11
breathing techniques, 52, 84, 167

Camus, A., 133
Carroll, L., 11
chakra system, 123-4
church, 16

defensiveness, 52, 92-3

educational system, 13
ego, 17

fear, 17, 93
Freud, S., 13, 91
Freudian Conscious, 91
  Ego, 91-4

Id, 91-2
Unconscious, 91, 93

Gallegos, Eligio Stephen, 152
Gestalt Psychology, 14
gestation, 156
Greece, 12
guilt, 45

Hillman, James, 15
history, 13
Humanness, 80
humour, 64-8

imagery, 13, 15, 17, 18, 52
imaginal, 15-17
imagination, 53, 85, 95

Jung, Carl, 13-15

language, 13, 16, 17
literature, 13
Locke, John, 12-13
logic, 13

loneliness, 84
love, 17, 43, 87-8

memory, 13, 52
mental illness, 67
Myth of Sisyphus, The, 133

Neihardt, John G., 169-72

objective observation, 12

phobias, 30
Popular Mechanix, 15
psychic surgery, 136-7

relationships, 109, 183
relaxation, 31, 63
   techniques, 52-3, 78
religions, 16, 30, 44
Renaissance, 12
Rennick, Teresa, 158

replicability, 12
Russia, 12

Schliemann, H., 15
self, relationship to body, 101-104
self concept, 17
sixth sense, 13
Skinner, B. F., 12
Sparta, 12
Swedenborg, E., 11

territory, 17
thinking, 17, 18
Troy, 15

United States, founders, 12

Van Gogh, V., 149

Watson, John B., 12
weight problems, 30-31